Routledge Revivals

A Study on the Minimum Wage

First Published in 1927, *A Study on the Minimum Wage* contains constructive proposals regarding the essential features of a satisfactory minimum wage system. Based on a comprehensive international study of existing legislation and practice in the 1920s, it brings crucial themes like objects of minimum wage legislation; the living wage; provisions for the worker's family; relation between the wages of men and women; machinery for fixing minimum wages; methods of enforcement; and the capacity of industry to pay. Rich in archival resources, this book is an essential read for students and researchers of labour history, labour economics, and political economy in general.

A Study on the Minimum Wage

J.H. Richardson

Routledge
Taylor & Francis Group

First published in 1927
by George Allen & Unwin Ltd

This edition first published in 2022 by Routledge
2 Park Square, Milton Park, Abingdon, Oxon, OX14 4RN
and by Routledge
605 Third Avenue, New York, NY 10017

Routledge is an imprint of the Taylor & Francis Group, an informa business

Publisher's Note
The publisher has gone to great lengths to ensure the quality of this reprint but
points out that some imperfections in the original copies may be apparent.

Disclaimer
The publisher has made every effort to trace copyright holders and welcomes
correspondence from those they have been unable to contact.

A Library of Congress record exists under LCCN: 27019232

ISBN: 978-1-032-18283-4 (hbk)
ISBN: 978-1-003-25378-5 (ebk)
ISBN: 978-1-032-18284-1 (pbk)

Book DOI 10.4324/9781003253785

A STUDY ON
THE MINIMUM WAGE

BY

J. H. RICHARDSON, M.A., B.Sc.(Econ.)

LONDON : GEORGE ALLEN & UNWIN LTD.
RUSKIN HOUSE, 40 MUSEUM STREET, W.C.1

First published in 1927

Printed in Great Britain by
Unwin Brothers, Ltd., Woking

PREFACE

TENTATIVE experiments in minimum wage regulation have been conducted in various countries during recent years. With the return of more stable economic conditions, demands will be made for extensions of such regulation. Instead of legislation protecting workers in a limited number of trades only, claims will be pressed for the fixing of minimum wages on a national basis. The present volume, which contains constructive proposals regarding the essential features of a satisfactory minimum wage system, may serve to indicate the practical possibilities in this direction, at the same time pointing out limitations and acting as a check to demands beyond the capacity of industry to pay.

The conclusions reached are based on a comprehensive international study of existing legislation and practice. For this study I have used the Library of the International Labour Office, which contains very complete information on the minimum wage systems of various countries. I have also had opportunities of discussing the special problems of each country with competent authorities. My thanks are particularly due to Dr. Karl Pribram, Chief of the Statistical Section of the International Labour Office, and to Mr. J. R. Bellerby for valuable advice and suggestions.

J. H. R.

GENEVA,
November 1926.

CONTENTS

A STUDY ON
THE MINIMUM WAGE

CHAPTER I

INTRODUCTION

RECOGNITION of the importance of social justice in labour conditions is a modern development. Under the feudal system conditions of labour were determined by status rather than by contract. The operation of the law of demand and supply was subject to considerable modification owing to the force of custom and the immobility of labour. Conditions were often regulated by law, but little thought was given to the welfare of the workers.

With the development of the modern industrial system in the eighteenth century and the adoption of *laissez-faire* principles, freedom of contract began to replace status and custom. Although the influence of custom persisted to some extent, and still serves to explain certain anomalies, especially as to the relation between the levels of wages in different trades, the law of demand and supply came to play a predominant part in determining conditions of labour. Any interference with free contract was considered economically unsound.

After a time, however, it became evident that

unrestrained competition led to intolerable evils. Excessive hours of labour, low wages, industrial accidents, and occupational diseases were among the consequences of the *laissez-faire* policy. From the middle of the nineteenth century workers' organisations developed, and these were able to secure improvements by means of collective agreements. Large numbers of workers, however, remained unorganised. These included women, juvenile workers, and also adult male workers in certain occupations, including homework trades. Attempts were made to organise such groups, but with little success.

The growth of public dissatisfaction with the consequences of an unrestricted policy of free competition led to demands for Government interference. Legislation for the protection of the workers became a necessity. By factory and other labour legislation, endeavours have been made to safeguard the workers against industrial accidents and diseases; excessive hours of labour have been prohibited and insurance schemes introduced to provide accident, sickness, and unemployment benefits. Many laws have been passed specially for the protection of women and children against the worst forms of exploitation.

The importance of securing improvements in labour conditions by legislative action was fully appreciated at Versailles by the authors of the Treaty of Peace. Recognising that the peace and harmony of the world are imperilled by the existence of hardship, injustice, and privation resulting from unsatisfactory conditions of labour, they set up the International Labour Organisation to assist in the maintenance of universal peace by establishing social justice for the workers. This organisation has, in fact, provided an effective stimulus to progress in labour legislation throughout a large part of the world, and has secured co-ordination and uniformity in the measures adopted in various countries.

In many countries, even in those with advanced labour legislation, minimum wage regulation has received little or no attention. Improvement in conditions of labour is, however, incomplete, and its value may be diminished unless steps are taken to secure to the workers the payment of a wage " adequate to maintain a reasonable standard of life." The benefits resulting from an increase in the amount of spare time which the worker has at his disposal in consequence of a diminution in the hours of labour are reduced if accompanied by a fall in wages which impairs his standard of living. More generally, if the cost of improving labour conditions is borne by the workers in terms of lower wages, then the progress effected may be more apparent than real. For *general* progress to be assured, therefore, a programme of labour legislation should include proposals for securing to the workers a reasonable minimum wage.

There is no essential difference in principle between fixing a minimum wage and fixing maximum hours of labour. Such limitations are among the rules regulating the conduct of industry, and a country which introduces any form of labour legislation has accepted the underlying principle involved. In no country is a complete *laissez-faire* attitude now adopted with regard to conditions of labour, and if the principle of interference is admitted, there is no logical reason for not dealing with the problem of wages.

Evidently in determining the rules according to which industry shall be conducted it is necessary to avoid imposing conditions which industry is unable to support. In the case of wages the difficulty lies in determining a minimum which safeguards the worker against privation, and which at the same time is within the capacity of industry to pay. Also, not only must the minimum be a practicable one, but a system of distribution must be retained which will give to workers with special skill a return sufficient to call forth an adequate supply of such labour, and will maintain the necessary supplies of capital, management, and other agents of production. Therein lies the real problem, one of the most difficult in the whole field of industry.

In attempting to find a solution, the chief factors to be considered are those affecting the capacity of industry to pay and those affecting the groups of workers for which wages are to be fixed. Improvement in the wages of the lowest paid grades of workers may be secured by an increase in the capacity of industry to pay, whether this be due to the introduction of more productive methods of manufacture or to an increase in the efficiency of the workers. It may also be effected by protecting the workers against exploitation and securing to them the highest wages that industry can afford to pay. In this connection the breaking down of traditional influences affecting adversely the wages of certain groups of workers is of importance. Thus the wages of women are often unduly low, partly on account of the limited field of labour hitherto open to them, and partly because many women have been willing to work for little remuneration as they were being maintained by the earnings of others.

During comparatively recent years, progress towards a solution of the problem has been made in certain countries by the adoption of various forms of minimum wage legislation.[1] The first minimum wage law was the New Zealand Industrial Conciliation and Arbitration Act of 1894, and subsequently the minimum wage principle has been widely adopted in English-speaking countries : Australia, Great Britain, the United States of America,[2] Canada, and South Africa. Other countries have applied the principle on a small scale, namely,

[1] An excellent critical survey of the minimum wage systems of different countries is given in *Wages and the State*, by Mrs. E. M. Burns, London, 1926. The present volume, based on independent original research, is similar in scope, but the method of treatment differs.

[2] The effectiveness of minimum wage legislation in the United States has been seriously impaired by recent decisions of the Supreme Court declaring the minimum wage laws of the District of Columbia and the State of Arizona to be unconstitutional.

France, Germany, Austria, Czechoslovakia, Norway, Hungary, the Argentine Republic, and Uruguay.

An examination of the minimum wage laws in force in these countries shows that in many cases only the fringe of the problem is being touched. Some laws are limited to special groups of workers, e.g. home-workers, female workers, agricultural workers. Even in Great Britain the legislation applies to workers in a limited number of trades, and for these the minimum rates are fixed independently by separate boards. The consequence is that unwarranted differences in rates may occur. Only in New Zealand and in certain Australian States have attempts been made to grapple with the whole problem.

Instead of legislation limited to a few trades, a system of general application is required. The writer is of opinion that as basis of the wage system of each country national minimum wages should be fixed.[1] These would constitute a standard below which no worker of ordinary ability should fall. They would provide the most effective means of preventing priva-tion and misery. In considering the basis to be adopted in determining the national minima, an attempt is made below to reconcile the apparently conflicting principles of the living wage and the capacity of industry to pay.

---

[1] In a country with several distinct economic regions, it might be necessary to adopt a regional instead of a national basis. Also different minima might be required for industrial and agricultural workers.

The family allowance system has often been advocated as a means of improving the welfare of the workers and their families. Therefore, this system must be examined in any study of minimum wage problems. The writer considers that, as a general rule, the adjustment of needs to income is preferable to the family allowance system of adjusting income to needs. However, in order to prevent misery, the family allowance system could, with advantage, be applied in occupations where wages are below the level considered reasonable in relation to the general standard of living of the community.

Among other problems which it has been necessary to discuss is that of the effect of international competition on the minimum wage standards of different countries. The standards of one nation may be undermined by the competition of others. To prevent this it is not necessary to attempt to secure the adoption of a uniform international minimum wage. Also such a solution is impracticable in view of existing differences in the levels of real wages in the various countries. What is required in order that progress in raising the minimum standards of any one country shall not be impeded is that other countries, on the basis of their own standards, shall advance at about the same rate.

CHAPTER II

OBJECTS OF MINIMUM WAGE LEGISLATION

THE objects of minimum wage legislation are various, and the basis on which rates are fixed, as well as the administrative machinery required, differs according to the purpose in view. One of the chief objects is the prevention of sweating. The development of organisation among the workers is sometimes mentioned as an indirect object of minimum wage legislation. A third object is the promotion of industrial peace.

PREVENTION OF SWEATING.

The most important purpose of minimum wage legislation is the raising of wages in industries where payment is unduly low. Such low payment may be the result of economic depression in the industry, inefficient organisation of production, inefficiency of the workers, or exploitation of labour. The economic conditions of industry are outside the control of minimum wage machinery. However, where an industry is in a state of permanent depression or, as a result of overcrowding, is unable to pay reasonable wages to all those seeking employment, the fixing of minimum wages at a reasonable level in relation to wages in other industries will hasten the transfer of workers to other employment, and thus lead to a better distribution of workers among the different industries. Such improved distribution would be secured by fixing general basic minima applicable to all industries.

Where low wages are due to inefficient organisation of production, any improvement which may result from the fixing of minimum wages is indirect. If it is possible to obtain workers at low wages, some employers will be careless in their use of labour. They will rely for their profits on a policy of employing a large number of workers under unsatisfactory conditions with antiquated machinery. If labour costs are high, greater attention will be devoted to the efficient organisation of the working force, since waste in this respect would mean heavy loss. The "economy" of high wages is thus likely to have favourable reactions on efficiency of management.[1] This in turn facilitates the payment of high wages.

[1] In *The Secret of High Wages*, by Bertram Austin and W. Francis Lloyd, London, 1926, the conclusion is reached that "High wages are an index of efficiency. Examples of enterprises are available in some of which wages are low, and in others wages are high. A careful examination into their condition cannot but reveal the truth that low wages are accompanied by low efficiency, and high wages with good efficiency."

Hamilton and May, in *The Control of Wages*, also make out a strong case for the payment of high wages, which they consider dependent largely on efficiency of management.

Estimates of the amount of waste in industry are given in the *Report of the Committee on Elimination of Waste in Industry appointed by the Federated American Engineering Societies*, New York, 1921.

B

The causes of inefficiency of the workers include lack of training and education, physical or mental defects, and poverty. The provision of facilities for education and vocational training falls outside the special field of activity of wage-fixing bodies. Workers suffering from physical or mental defect would find difficulty in securing employment if employers were required to pay the same wage rate to them as to workers of ordinary ability. Therefore a number of minimum wage laws make provision for the fixing of lower rates for handicapped than for ordinary workers. These provisions are examined in a later chapter. As regards poverty, minimum wage machinery is concerned mainly with the wage element on the income side of the worker's budget. It was seen above that the wage may be unduly low owing to depression in the industry. Such a wage may also be the result of exploitation.

Exploitation of labour may be defined as taking advantage of the inferior bargaining power of the workers to pay them a lower wage than that justified by the economic value of their work. But the worker's productive capacity is impaired by wages insufficient for reasonable subsistence, and this evil tends to be perpetuated owing to the impossibility of supplying the needs of his children. Consequently exploitation may cause the productive capacity of the worker to fall to the level of the wage paid. It is one of the objects of minimum wage machinery to prevent exploitation and to endeavour to restore the efficiency of workers whose productive capacity has been reduced by exploitation.

To prevent the payment of wages lower than the economic value of the work done is comparatively easy. Such exploitation is mainly the result of weakness in bargaining power on the part of the workers. Minimum wage machinery, by establishing greater equality of bargaining power, can ensure the payment of a wage which corresponds closely with the productive capacity of the worker. In doing so there is no danger of causing unemployment, since the worker is worth the wage fixed. Where exploitation has impaired the productive capacity of the workers, the problem is more difficult. To raise wages considerably would endanger their employment. Therefore, wages must be improved gradually, particularly when trade is prosperous. The increases in wages will be likely to result in an increase in the efficiency of the workers, and also in that of the workers of the future through improvement in the health and welfare of the children. It will thus have a beneficial effect on production, which will be, within limits, cumulative. Where this result is obtained, the increase in wages will involve no ultimate burden either on the employers or the consumers of the goods produced, but will be covered by the increased productivity of the workers themselves.

The importance of preventing exploitation is increased by the fact that, if certain employers exploit their workers, competition makes it difficult for other employers to maintain fair wages. As has been seen above, a policy of cutting wage rates tends to divert attention from the securing of profits by means of efficient organisation to the attaining of this end at the expense of labour, and in most industries there are some employers who find this policy the easier course.[1] It is evidently an advantage to employers who desire to pay a fair wage if such a practice be prevented.

From the point of view of these employers interest centres not on the establishment of general minima applicable to all industries, but on the fixing within any given industry of minimum scales of wages for the different grades of workers. The problem is one of wage standardisation, the essential feature being that for each grade a minimum should be fixed below which no establishment would be allowed to fall.[2]

Wage standardisation is of interest also to the

---

[1] Thus, with regard to Ontario, it is stated in the *Third Annual Report of the Minimum Wage Board*, 1923, p. 3: "We have found no 'sweated' trades, but we have found 'sweated' plants in practically every trade. In some trades there are very few such plants. In other trades there are more, and no trade is without at least one or two."

[2] The fixing of minimum wages does not imply complete standardisation, since employers and workers are free to agree on higher wages, and consequently variations are likely to be found. In so far, however, as the minima are effective, i.e. are actually paid in a number of establishments, a measure of standardisation is introduced.

Where various grades of skilled workers are concerned, the problem ceases to be one of preventing sweating in the sense in which the term is commonly understood, i.e. including privation resulting from low wages.

workers quite apart from the prevention of poverty. In many industries there is a high degree of standardisation of productive processes. It is evidently unsatisfactory if workers performing similar work under similar conditions receive different rates of remuneration, rates varying according to the relative bargaining power of the workers and employers, or the profitableness of different undertakings.[1] In other words, the problem is that of applying the principle of "equal pay for equal work."

Somewhat similar is the idea of ensuring a given minimum to piece-rate workers. The earnings of such workers may sometimes fall to an exceptionally low level owing to circumstances outside their control. The mining industry furnishes typical examples. Thus, a coal-hewer, who is generally paid according to the number of tons he extracts, may during certain periods extract only a small quantity of coal owing to difficulties encountered in the place where he is working. In consequence the earnings to which he is entitled at ruling piece rates may be low. The work he has done, perhaps of a preparatory character, may, however, be of equal value to that of a worker who, on account of the facility of extraction at the face where he has been working, has a large quantity of coal to his credit. There are various ways of

---

[1] The demand of the coal-miners in Great Britain in 1921, and subsequently, for a national instead of a district agreement is in part based on the principle that similar work in different districts should be paid for at similar rates.

making allowance for difficult workings,[1] and amongst these perhaps the most satisfactory is to guarantee a minimum time wage. The demand for such a minimum, as a protection to miners working in abnormal places, played a considerable part in the agitation which preceded the adoption of the Coal Mines (Minimum Wage) Act of 1912 in Great Britain, although other arguments were also used, including that for a living wage.[2]

DEVELOPMENT OF ORGANISATION.

The payment of unduly low wages, especially where caused by the cutting of rates by certain employers, could be largely prevented by means of organised action on the part of the workers. A strong trade union would be able to prevent wages in individual establishments from falling considerably below the general level, and would also be able to secure the highest rates which the industry could bear.[3] This

---

[1] For example, when determining wage rates for work in any given place, account may be taken of its special conditions, but consideration of this kind is largely dependent on the sympathy and good will of the manager.

[2] Another argument used for a general minimum time wage for underground workers was that, if a worker is justified in claiming a minimum time wage while working under abnormal natural conditions, he is equally justified in demanding a minimum time wage if his earnings are low owing to faulty management (e.g. lack of tubs). For the effects of the Act see H. S. Jevons, *The British Coal Trade*, p. 599; also J. W. F. Rowe, *Wages in the Coal Industry*, p. 110.

[3] See H. Clay, "The Post-war Wages Problem," a paper read

is to a large extent true, but it is frequently in those industries in which the workers are badly organised that the level of wages is unduly low, and that in certain establishments serious exploitation is found. It is to protect unorganised or badly organised workers that the minimum wage principle has been applied in certain countries. The fixing of wages by machinery established by law is regarded as necessary while the workers remain badly organised, but if trade union organisation should develop sufficiently, the application of the law would be suspended, and wages determined by the ordinary process of collective bargaining.

The principle of State interference only in cases where wages cannot be regulated adequately by collective agreement is given recognition in the minimum wage laws of a number of countries, including Austria, Czechoslovakia, Germany, and Norway. In Great Britain the Minister of Labour has power to withdraw any trade from the operation of the Trade Boards Acts if organisation becomes adequate for the effective regulation of wages.

In Australasia the development of organisation

before Section F of the British Association, Liverpool, September 1923, printed in the *Economic Journal*, March 1924, p. 6 : " An organised trade is likely to secure a higher rate than an unorganised one would in circumstances otherwise similar ; standard rates will have a wider authority and be more uniformly observed where the organisation extends over the whole of a trade and is not confined to a few favoured districts. Organisation is a condition of obtaining the highest wage that the trade at any moment will bear."

among workers and employers has been encouraged
by various laws establishing wage-fixing machinery.
Thus in New Zealand the Industrial Conciliation and
Arbitration Act of 1894 and its amending Acts have
provided a stimulus to the growth of organisations.
Neither the individual workman nor the individual
employer is recognised under the law, except in so
far as he is a member of a registered union, and disputes
can be brought before the Councils of Conciliation or
the Court of Arbitration only by registered unions of
workers or associations of employers. In this case,
however, as in similar cases in Australian States, the
object was not so much to secure the development
of organisation so that wages might be regulated
satisfactorily by collective agreement as to ensure the
regular working of the arbitration system for settling
disputes.

The Trade Boards system is sometimes regarded as
a means of stimulating the development of organisation. Boards composed of an equal number of representatives of employers and of workers, together with
one or more disinterested persons, are set up in each
trade. Where a proportion of employers or workers
in a trade are organised, these are invited to nomi-
nate representatives. The number of workers' or
of employers' representatives thus nominated often
bears the same proportion to the total number of
workers' or employers' representatives as the number
of organised workers or employers in the trade bears
to the total number of workers or employers in the

trade. Members representing unorganised workers or employers are selected by the Government department responsible for the administration of the legislation. It is considered that the right to make nominations according to the membership of the organisation, and the greater influence on the board of a representative of an organisation than of a member representing unorganised workers or employers, will lead to a development of organisation. On the other hand, the argument is advanced that the chief purpose of a Trade Union is the improvement of wages and other conditions of labour, and that this constitutes the main reason for workers joining the unions. If minimum wage machinery set up by law be effective in improving conditions, many workers may consider it unnecessary to join an organisation.

In practice the development of organisation does not appear to have been seriously considered as an object of minimum wage legislation. Any effects are therefore indirect. The information available leads to the conclusion that, although the setting up of minimum wage fixing machinery has led in certain cases to a strengthening of the organisation of workers and employers, the improvement has been small. This is largely because minimum wage machinery has often been established in trades in which organisation is difficult, especially on the workers' side. The development of strong organisations is especially hard to effect among homeworkers and workers in small scale undertakings. Also difficulties have been encountered

in organising women workers in certain trades.[1]
In such cases the growth of strong organisations of
workers is unlikely, and the need for minimum wage
regulation may be regarded as of a permanent rather
than of a transitional character.

PROMOTION OF INDUSTRIAL PEACE.

In industries with powerful organisations of employers and workers, wages can usually be regulated,
more or less satisfactorily, by collective agreement.
However, agreement is not always possible, and disputes
may result in a cessation of work, causing serious
dislocation in the economic life of the community.   In
certain countries laws have been passed for the purpose of removing this danger.   One method is to
make strikes and lockouts illegal.   The prohibition of
strikes takes away one of the weapons of the workers
for improving their conditions.   When, therefore, the
State adopts this course, it must provide a satisfactory alternative system of wage regulation.   The
system employed is generally that of arbitration.
Where arbitration machinery is established, disputes
involving wage issues call for the fixing of minimum
rates of wages for different categories of workers by
an arbitrator, or an Arbitration Court.

[1] About 70 per cent. of workers under the British Trade
Boards Acts are women.   In the United States and Canada
the minimum wage principle has been applied almost entirely
to women workers, while in various countries of continental
Europe the minimum wage system has been adopted for
homeworkers only.

In Australia and New Zealand one of the main objects of minimum wage regulation is the prevention of industrial disputes. The Arbitration Courts are often less concerned with low-paid, unorganised workers than with various grades of strongly organised workers. In order that similar awards may be given in similar disputes, an Arbitration Court must adopt general principles of wage regulation. These principles have often been applied by employers and workers in their own direct negotiations, and have facilitated the reaching of agreement without recourse to the court.

To sum up, minimum wage fixing machinery, by preventing undue differences between the minimum rates of wages for work of similar difficulty in different industries, facilitates the most satisfactory distribution of workers. At the same time poverty resulting from unduly low wages in industries seriously over-crowded or permanently depressed is avoided. The fixing of minimum rates of wages may also prevent exploitation of workers. Reactions on the efficiency of the workers and on the efficiency of productive organisation are important. The establishment of certain types of minimum wage fixing machinery may lead to the growth of workers' unions and employers' associations; however, no very marked development is to be anticipated. Arbitration Courts for the settlement of disputes are mainly concerned with the making of awards for well-organised workers.

From the foregoing it is evident that for a complete system of minimum wage regulation two kinds of minimum wages should be fixed : (1) minima to prevent sweating among the lowest paid groups of workers in the community ; (2) minima for higher paid groups of workers. In the present study, although reference is made to both types of minima and to each of the objects indicated above, attention is directed especially to the problem of fixing minima to protect the lowest paid groups of workers. With this main object in view, the various bases on which minimum wages may be fixed are now examined.

CHAPTER III

BASES ADOPTED IN DIFFERENT COUNTRIES

MINIMUM wage laws differ considerably with regard to the bases or criteria adopted for fixing the wage rates. The basis on which the rates are fixed is of primary importance where the object is to prevent sweating, or to promote industrial peace. If the purpose of a law be to stimulate the growth of organisation, and thus prepare the way for the satisfactory regulation of wages by the ordinary processes of collective bargaining, the basis on which the wages are fixed is of less importance than the machinery for fixing. The basis is also of secondary importance where the object is to prevent unfair competition between employers, as here the essential condition is the standardisation of rates.

For the prevention of sweating, certain laws make provision for the fixing of an adequate living wage; others base the minimum rates for one group of workers on the wages paid to other groups, while some laws give no indication as to the rates that should be paid, but merely provide for the setting up of machinery for fixing minimum rates. In the last case, wage fixing authorities are free to fix the rates on whatever basis they consider most satisfactory. In practice, authorities either adopt one of the bases already mentioned or attempt to secure the highest

wage that the industry under consideration can afford
to pay. Where the object is to promote industrial
peace, the living wage principle is generally accepted,
at least nominally. But the rigid application of this
principle alone may fail to lead to a settlement in any
given dispute. Therefore, in practice, it has been
found necessary to introduce further principles, e.g.
the capacity of industry to pay.[1]

There are thus three main bases for fixing minimum
wages :

1. The relation to the wages of other categories of
   workers ;
2. The living wage ;
3. The capacity of industry to pay.

Under these headings the present chapter surveys
the bases adopted in the legislation of various countries.
Certain laws, in which more than one basis is indicated,
are classified according to the chief basis.

Relation to the Wages of Other Categories of Workers.[2]

Minimum wages for a given category of workers
may be fixed in relation to the wages of workers in

---

[1] Mr. Justice Higgins, President of the Australian Commonwealth Court of Arbitration, in declaring an award, emphasised
that an Arbitration Court has primarily to settle disputes, and
said : " If I cannot manage to keep the wheels of industry
moving except by awarding less or more than the ideal minimum, I might be justified in making such an award."

[2] The fair-wage clause, which, in many countries, forms

allied trades, or to the average wages paid in a large number of other industries. The standard in the first case is limited to the wages paid in a few similar trades, while, in the second, the general level of wages in the district or country is taken as basis.

In France, under the Homework Act of 1915, the minimum rates of female homeworkers in the clothing trades are based on the earnings of factory workers making similar articles. In Norway the Homework Act of 1918 provides that the minimum rates of homeworkers in the trades covered shall be fixed in relation to wages current in the locality for similar work done in factories, or in relation to the wages of homeworkers in other trades. It is further provided that the minimum rates are to be fixed in such relation to wages in workshops and factories that homework shall not be displaced.[1] The German Homework Act of 1923 follows similar lines.

Where minimum wages are determined in relation to the rates paid to workers in the same or allied trades they are generally fixed at a level which differs little, if at all, from those rates. For homeworkers engaged on piece-work there is no reason why, other things being equal, their piece rates should differ

part of the provisions of public contracts, often stipulates that the wages paid by contractors shall not be less than the standard, trade union, or other fair rate paid in the district in which the contract work is performed. In some cases the wages are not to be below those paid by good or reputable employers.

[1] This implies a consideration of capacity to pay.

from those paid to factory workers who make similar articles. On the market the articles will sell for the same price, whether they are made by homeworkers or factory workers. In such cases the principle of "equal pay for equal work" should apply. Where other things are not equal, e.g. where the cost of distribution and control of work in respect of home-workers exceeds that of factory workers, or where the quality of the work differs, allowance may be necessary. Thus, in Great Britain and in Norway, the wages of homeworkers have been fixed, in certain cases, slightly below those of factory workers.

A levelling-up of wages in some branches of a trade to those paid in other branches or in allied trades may lead to little improvement. Workers in the whole group of allied trades under consideration may be in receipt of wages well below those paid to similar grades of workers in most other industries. Their relatively unsatisfactory situation may be a conse-quence of the economic condition of the industry or the result of exploitation. In either case it is desirable to consider the relation between the wages paid in any one industry and the general level of wages.

Where minimum rates are to be fixed in relation to the general level of wages paid to workers of corre-sponding skill in different industries, it is necessary first to determine the general or average level. The average of wages paid in a number of industries would generally be unsatisfactory as the minimum rate for a given industry. The average is based on a range of wages in different industries and establishments, some of which are below, and some above, the average level. Apart from special conditions, the minimum for a given industry must be below the general average, e.g. 80 per cent. of the average.

Two main reasons may be distinguished for fixing the minimum wage of a given group of workers in relation to the wages paid to other workers. First, differences in standards of living are reduced by raising the wages of the group under consideration more nearly to those of other groups of workers. In any community, one of the chief tests of the adequacy or inadequacy of the wages of a given group of workers is comparison with those of other groups, and if extreme differences are avoided the public conscience is usually satisfied. The second reason is that if a number of industries or establishments can afford to pay a given rate of wages, then others may reasonably be called on to pay wages which are not widely divergent from them. At the basis, therefore, of the method of fixing the wages of certain groups of workers in relation to those of other groups is either the standard of living principle or that of capacity to pay.

THE LIVING WAGE BASIS.

In New Zealand, most of the Australian States, and in a number of States or Provinces in the United States and in Canada, the living wage, defined in various terms, is taken as the basis on which mini-

mum wages are fixed. In certain laws references to
the living wage are accompanied by qualifications
which may undermine or destroy their value. For
example, the Massachusetts Minimum Wage Act
provides that the financial condition of the occupation,
as well as the needs of the workers, shall be taken
into consideration in fixing minimum rates. Such
laws are dealt with later under the heading of the
Capacity of Industry to Pay.

In New Zealand the law specifies no basis, but, in
practice, in making an award the Arbitration Court
takes into account the economic and financial conditions affecting trade and industry, and all other
relevant circumstances, but will in no case "reduce
wages below a fair standard of living wage." The
basic principle is, therefore, that of the living wage.

The Australian Commonwealth Arbitration Court
has played an important part in the development of
principles for the fixing of minimum wages. Although
not laid down in the statute which set up the Court,
the living wage basis has, in practice, been adopted.
The Court makes its awards for unskilled adult male
workers in accordance with the requirements, in a
civilised community, of a man with wife and three
children. The basic rate thus determined must be
paid regardless of the effects on an individual industry
or establishment. The condition of the industry may,
on the other hand, affect "secondary minima," i.e.
the higher wages to be paid to skilled workers.

In the State of South Australia the Industrial

Arbitration Act, 1912, provides that a living wage shall be fixed " sufficient for the normal and reasonable needs of the average employee living in the locality where the work under consideration is done or is to be done." By the Western Australian Industrial Arbitration Act, 1912, the wages fixed shall be sufficient " to enable the average worker to whom it applies to live in reasonable comfort, having regard to any domestic obligations to which such average workman would be ordinarily subject." The New South Wales law defines the " domestic obligations " to be taken into consideration in fixing the wages of adult male workers. The Industrial Commission is charged with the duty of declaring at regular intervals the cost of living for a man with wife and two children under fourteen years of age, and this amount becomes the basic rate for adult male workers. The wage is based on the requirements of the worker and his family as members of a civilised community which has resolved, so far as the law can do it, that competition shall not be allowed to lead to sweated conditions. The minimum wage for adult female workers is based on the requirements of a woman maintaining herself by means of her work, but without dependants.

The Queensland Industrial Arbitration Act of 1916 gives special indications as to the basis to be considered by the Board of Trade and Arbitration in fixing wages. " The minimum wages of an adult male employee shall be not less than is sufficient to maintain a well-conducted employee of average health, strength, and competence, and his wife and a family of three children in a fair and average standard of comfort, having regard to the conditions of living prevailing among employees in the calling in respect of which such minimum wage is fixed, and provided that in fixing such minimum wage the earnings of the children or wife of such employee shall not be taken into account." The qualification "having regard to the conditions of living prevailing in the calling" is also added with regard to the wages of adult female employees. The conditions of living of workers in any trade are determined mainly by the wages paid in that trade. Therefore, the minimum rates are to be fixed on the basis of the wages paid in the trade prior to the fixing of such rates. Wages in the trade are not necessarily adequate to provide a standard of living which would be considered satisfactory in relation to the general standards of the community as a whole. They need not even be equal to the capacity of the industry to pay, but merely what the industry is actually paying.[1]

In the United States, in most States which have passed minimum wage laws, the legislation provides, with slight variations in phraseology, that the minimum rates fixed must be adequate to supply the workers with the necessary cost of living, and to maintain their

---

[1] In practice a given sum (£4 5s. per week in August 1924) has been declared as the minimum weekly wage for unskilled workers in normal industries of average prosperity. The right is reserved to fix lower minima in industries unable to sustain that rate, and higher minima in industries more prosperous than the average.

health and welfare. In Minnesota the wage must be sufficient to provide the necessary comforts and conditions of a reasonable life.[1] The bodies charged with the determination of minimum rates generally take as a basis budgets of commodities which are considered necessary for maintenance of health and welfare. In some cases rates have been fixed below the amount necessary to purchase the budget. This has been because, although the wage-fixing body considered the rates inadequate, it seemed impossible to get employers to agree to the wage regarded by the fixing authority as adequate.[2]

In most of the Provinces of Canada which have passed minimum wage laws the rates fixed must be adequate to supply the necessary cost of living.

In both the United States and Canada, where minimum wage laws apply mainly to women, the living wage for experienced workers is fixed at the amount considered necessary for a worker supporting herself but without dependants.

CAPACITY OF INDUSTRY TO PAY.

It has been seen that where minimum rates are to be fixed in relation to the wages of other groups of

---

[1] Reference has already been made to the Massachusetts law under which account must be taken of the financial condition of the occupation.

[2] United States Department of Labor, Bureau of Labor Statistics, Bulletin 369 : *The Use of Cost of Living Figures in Wage Adjustments*, by Elma B. Carr, Washington, May 1925, pp. 156–99.

workers, the purpose may be to ensure that the rates
are within the capacity of industry to pay. Some
minimum wage laws specifically state that, in fixing
the minimum rates, account must be taken of the
capacity of industry to pay. Thus, by the Massachusetts Minimum Wage Act, the Trade Boards which
recommend the rates to be fixed for different categories
of workers are directed to take into consideration not
only the needs of the workers, but also " the financial
condition of the occupation and the probable effect
thereon of any increase of wages paid." In applying
this Act the dominant factor has been the living
wage principle, although, especially in times of depressed trade, wages below those considered necessary
to supply essential requirements have been fixed in
certain industries which were believed unable to pay
the living wage.[1]

The British Trade Boards Acts give no guidance
to the Boards as to the basis they should adopt when
fixing minimum rates.[2] Consequently when, in 1922,
the Cave Committee made its enquiry into the working
and effects of the Acts, considerable diversity was
found. In its report the Committee state that some
boards had taken account only of the cost of living,
while others had taken into consideration the value

[1] United States Department of Labor, Bureau of Labor
Statistics, Bulletin No. 285, *Minimum Wage Laws of the
United States : Construction and Operation*, p. 121.

[2] This is true also of the Austrian and Czechoslovakian
Homework Acts, and of the minimum wage laws of one or
two States in the United States and Provinces in Canada.

of the work done, and the charge which the trade could bear. " In one case we are informed that the minimum was taken to be the lowest wage payable to the least skilled worker in the cheapest living area covered by the rate ; while in another it was defined as a wage sufficient to provide a young woman of eighteen with means sufficient to enable her to maintain herself without assistance, and to enable a man of twenty-one to contemplate marriage." [1]

When the Cave Committee framed its recommendations, it proposed that the Trade Boards System should be directed " to give protection to the workers in each trade by securing to them at least a wage which approximates to the subsistence level in the place in which they live and which the trade can bear." There was thus, as in the Massachusetts Act, an attempt to combine the principle of the living wage and that of the capacity of industry to pay. The wage which a given trade can bear may, however, be lower than that which would be recognised as a subsistence wage.

The British Agricultural Wages Act of 1924 recognises the living wage principle. The Committees set up under the Act are charged with the duty of securing, as far as practicable, for able-bodied men such wages as are adequate to promote efficiency and to enable a man to maintain himself and his family in accordance

---

[1] *Report to the Minister of Labour of the Committee Appointed to Enquire into the Working and Effects of the Trade Boards Acts*, Cd. 1645, London, 1922,

with a reasonable standard of comfort. The qualification " as far as practicable " implies that the fixing
of a living wage is not obligatory. The capacity of
industry to pay is the real basis.

The State of Victoria Factories and Shops Act, 1915,
resembles the British Trade Boards legislation as regards the basis on which minimum rates are to be fixed.
No definite guidance is given to the Trade Boards set
up by the Act, although it is suggested that they
should not fix " the very lowest amount reasonably
consistent with existence, but endeavour to determine
what is a fair wage, taking account of conditions of a
permanent character." [1] The Court of Industrial Appeals, in dealing with objections to rates fixed by Boards,
must consider " whether the determination appealed
against has had, or may have, the effect of prejudicing
the progress, maintenance of, or scope of employment
in the trade or industry affected by any such price
or rate ; and, if of opinion that it has, or may have,
such effect, the Court shall make such alteration as,
in its opinion, may be necessary to remove or prevent
such effect, and, at the same time, to secure a living

[1] Some regard must be had also to the wages of other
groups of workers. Thus the Boards are warned that wages
in any given trade should not be increased if they compare
favourably with wages paid in other trades in Victoria, or
with those paid in the same trade in other States. From
1903 to 1907 each Board was to base the wages it fixed on
the rates actually paid by reputable employers to workers
of average ability in the trade. This basis resembled that
adopted in the fair-wages clauses of Government contracts
in various countries.

wage to the employees in such trade or industry."
As already indicated, however, certain industries
may be unable to pay what is considered to be a
living wage.

Under the present heading may be mentioned a
closely related basis to which reference is sometimes
made, namely, the value of the work done. If wages
are fixed in accordance with this basis, they are clearly
within the capacity of industry to pay. In fact, the
two bases are practically identical, and one method
of determining capacity to pay would be to find the
value of the work done. Under modern conditions of
mass production, with specialised labour, it is difficult
to determine the value to the employer of the work
done by a group of workers in relation to that by other
groups. The value of the work done by all the workers
engaged in the manufacture of a given product, in
relation to the value added by capital and management, is at least equally difficult to estimate.

Of the three bases considered above, that of relation
to the wages of other categories of workers was seen
to be dependent, according to the point of view, either
on the living wage principle or on that of the capacity
of industry to pay. These last two principles are more
fundamental, and appear to be conflicting. They are
therefore examined in some detail in the three following
chapters, and an attempt is made to show the extent
to which they may be reconciled.

CHAPTER IV

THE LIVING WAGE

THE purpose of the present chapter is to show the elastic character of the living wage and its dependence on the wealth of the community. An attempt is made to deduce certain general principles which should be applied if the living wage is adopted as basis in fixing minimum wages. Before, however, dealing with these questions, the methods which may be adopted in order to determine the amount of a living wage are considered.

METHODS OF DETERMINING A LIVING WAGE.

The real wage of the worker consists of the quantities of food, housing accommodation, clothing, fuel, lighting, and other commodities which he can buy with his money wage. Consequently, in many investigations to determine a living wage, a budget of necessary commodities is first compiled. The money cost of the budget is then calculated at ruling prices, and this sum declared to be the living wage.

The commodity budget may be determined either by the theoretical method or by the family budget enquiry method. According to the theoretical method, in the case of food, estimates are made of the number of calories required by adults of either sex, and also by children of different ages. Analysis of different kinds of food shows the number of calories contained in a given quantity of each, and a budget is drawn up which will provide the number of calories needed by an individual, or by a family of given size. For housing, the amount of accommodation is determined mainly according to the number of cubic feet of air space required for the preservation of health. Estimates for other groups of expenditure are based on the habits of the workers, and not on theoretical considerations. Thus the method is incomplete, as its application is limited to food and housing accommodation. Even for food the method is defective. People do not, in fact, determine their food consumption according to the caloric value of different commodities. Also a given number of calories may be provided either by a few cheap articles of food, e.g. rye bread, potatoes, margarine, or by a varied diet of expensive commodities. For use in determining a living wage, therefore, the theoretical method is of little value.

The family budget enquiry method is more satisfactory. From an adequate number of representative families, information is obtained as to the actual quantities of different commodities consumed during a given period, together with the cost and quality of their housing accommodation. The results are based on actual conditions, not on hypothetical considerations. Since each class of the community has its own standard of living, the results of family budget enquiries vary according to the class from which the data are obtained. Information as to the budgets of the families of unskilled workers is the more useful guide for fixing a minimum or basic wage.

In compiling a commodity budget as basis for a living wage there appears to be a tendency to adopt a higher standard of living than that attained by large numbers of unskilled workers. Investigators, when determining what they consider to be an " adequate " standard, find it difficult to omit from the budget many commodities which are, in fact, beyond the reach of large sections of the community. The danger of adopting too high a standard is lessened if the family budgets of unskilled workers are taken as basis, but even where this course is followed there is a tendency to make use of the budgets of families above the lowest level of this class. If improvements are to be effected, it is necessary to adopt a standard higher than that of the least fortunate members of the community. How much higher must be decided arbitrarily by the authority responsible for determining the living wage. It is this unavoidable arbitrary element which is the chief defect of the living wage principle.

THE ELASTIC CHARACTER OF THE LIVING WAGE.

The element of elasticity cannot be removed from definitions of a living wage, and such words as " adequate " or " reasonable " are essentially vague.[1]

[1] In the *Second Annual Report of the District of Columbia Minimum Wage Board* (1919), p. 18, is the following passage : " The cost of living is such an unstandardised subject that a mathematically accurate determination is impossible. In

By whatever method the living wage is determined, the result varies according to the point of view of the investigator. An examination of living wage estimates made, whether by private investigators or public authorities, shows considerable variation in the results obtained in different enquiries. The elastic character of the living wage and the different standards adopted by various investigators may be illustrated by reference to a number of typical enquiries in three countries in which special attention has been directed to the problem—namely, Great Britain, the United States, and Australia.[1]

Great Britain.

Among the best-known researches into the cost of living of low-paid wage-earners are those of Mr. B. Seebohm Rowntree.[2] Two different studies were made, the first of which resulted in an estimate of requirements for mere physical efficiency. This was

each conference there are as many different opinions as there are members. In general, the employers want a wage sufficient to maintain existing standards of living in the industry, while the employees contend that the standard of living should be improved. The wage finally agreed upon is not a scientific determination based solely on facts, but rather a compromise of opinion between the two groups, modified, as it may be, by the opinion of the public."

[1] Direct comparison between estimates in different countries is largely valueless owing to differences in the purchasing power of money. In a later section, certain international comparisons are drawn in which allowance is made for such inequalities.

[2] See *Poverty : a Study of Town Life* ; also *The Human Needs of Labour*.

based on statistics of actual consumption in York, which was regarded as being roughly representative of towns in England. The second study had as object the determination of a somewhat higher but still meagre standard of human needs, not a standard that is desirable, but one below which no class of worker should ever be forced to live. This standard was based on enquiries among working people as to their expenditure on necessaries, although, in the case of food, account was taken of nutritive requirements and a dietary drawn up to meet them. Separate estimates were made of the requirements per week of a man with wife and three children, and of a woman living alone without dependants. The figures according to the two standards at the level of prices in 1914, together with corresponding data for January 1926 calculated by allowing for changes in the cost of living, were as follows :—

	1914.		January 1926.	
	s.	d.	s.	d.
For a man with wife and three children—				
(a) For mere physical efficiency	26	0	45	6
(b) For human needs..	35	3	61	8
For a single woman living alone—				
(a) For mere physical efficiency	16	0	28	0
(b) For human needs..	20	0	35	0

The figures for January 1926 may be compared with the minimum rates of wages fixed by Trade Boards for male and female workers in Great Britain.[1] At the beginning of 1926 the averages of minimum

[1] The figures are based on data published in the *Eighteenth Abstract of Labour Statistics* (Cd. 2740, London, 1926), p. 109. The rate for adults is generally paid to women of eighteen years of age and over, and to men of twenty-one years and over.

rates for the lowest paid class of experienced adult
workers in about forty different trades were :—

	Per Hour.		Per Week of 48 Hours.	
	s.	d.	s.	d.
Males	1	0½	50	0
Females	0	7	28	0

Thus the wage rates of both males and females were
considerably below Mr. Rowntree's estimates for
human needs, although they were equal to or slightly
above the level for mere physical efficiency, i.e. the
poverty line.[1] With regard to workers not covered
by Trade Boards, the wages of skilled workers in the
shipbuilding and engineering industries were slightly
below the standard of human needs ; skilled building
trade workers, printers, bookbinders, and furniture
makers were distinctly above it, while unskilled
labourers in the engineering and shipbuilding industries
were below the poverty line.[2]

[1] In the case of adult male workers a considerable number
would have fewer dependants than those covered by Mr.
Rowntree's estimates, and would, in consequence, be better off.

[2] According to data published in the *Labour Gazette*, October
1925, the average wage rates of these categories of workers
at the end of September 1925 were :—

Skilled workers—		Per Week.		
		s.	d.	s.	d.
Building trade, printing, bookbinding, and furniture making .. about		73	0 to 74	0
Engineering		56	0 to 61	0
Shipbuilding		55	0 to 58	0
Unskilled workers—				
Engineering and shipbuilding, about		38	6 to 40	0

Changes between September 1925 and January 1926 were
insignificant.

United States.

Many commodity budgets and estimates of the cost of living have been established in the United States. They cover standards ranging from the poverty line to a high level of comfort. Of the latter type is the minimum quantity budget drawn up by the United States Bureau of Labor Statistics under the direction of Dr. Royal Meeker.[1] It is based on requirements to maintain a worker's family of five persons in health and decency, according to American ideas. The food quantities, which supply about 3,500 calories per adult man, are based on the actual consumption of 280 families in the United States, modifications being made to ensure the right proportions of proteins, fats, and carbohydrates. The articles of clothing provide for the physical needs of warmth, cleanliness, and comfort, and are of reasonably good quality. They are based on the clothing budgets of about 850 families. In the case of housing a standard of one room per person is adopted, together with bathroom, hall, etc., the area of the whole dwelling totalling 660 square feet. The requirements for heat, artificial light, furniture, furnishings, and miscellaneous items are also specified in detail.

The budget is constructed from the actual consumption of various families selected largely because they had attained what was considered a reasonable standard. In fact, it represents a standard attainable in

[1] United States Bureau of Labor Statistics, *Monthly Labor Review*, June 1920.

the United States by skilled workers, but out of the reach of most unskilled workers. Unfortunately, no estimate is available of the cost of this budget, although Dr. Meeker, in a paper to the American Public Health Association, December 1918, claimed that family schedules obtained in Washington in 1916 showed the minimum amount required to maintain in comfort a family consisting of husband, wife, and three children under fifteen years of age, to be at least $1,150 per annum.[1] At the level of prices at the beginning of 1926 this was equal to about $1,700 to $1,800 per annum, or about $32½ to $34½ per week.

Other American estimates are tabulated below, together with the equivalent costs at the beginning of 1926.[2] The figure obtained by the New York City Board of Estimate and Apportionment was the result of an investigation conducted to provide a basis for standardising the wages of unskilled workers employed by the city authorities. The amount estimated was to supply the requirements, according to American ideas, of a family of two adults and three children under fourteen years of age. The result of the investigation corresponds closely with Mr. Ogburn's estimate of the cost of a minimum standard of living in New York City at the American subsistence level.

[1] This standard appears to be somewhat lower than that of the minimum quantity budget.

[2] Summaries of the investigations on which these and other estimates were based are given in *Family Budgets of American Wage-earners*, by the National Industrial Conference Board (Research Report, No. 41).

D

ESTIMATES OF THE COST OF LIVING FOR A FAMILY OF FIVE ACCORDING TO VARIOUS STANDARDS.

Authority and Standard.	Estimates.		Approximate Equivalent at Beginning of 1926.	
	Place and Date.	Amount per Annum.	Per Annum.	Per Week.
		Dollars.	Dollars.	Dollars.
New York City Board of Estimate and Apportionment—				
Minimum for unskilled workers ..	New York, Feb. 1915	844·94	1,500	29·0
Mr. William F. Ogburn [1]—				
Minimum of subsistence .. : :	New York, July 1918	1,386	1,580	30·0
Minimum of comfort .. : :	New York, July 1918	1,760·50	2,000	38·5
Professor Paul H. Douglas [2]—				
Poverty line	Chief cities, 1925 ..	1,000–1,100	1,000–1,100	20·0

[1] These estimates were made for the National War Labor Board on the basis of data collected by the United States Bureau of Labor Statistics with regard to shipbuilding workers in New York.

[2] Professor Douglas also gives the following estimates for a family of five at the level of prices in 1925 on the basis of the results of investigations conducted by various persons :—

	Dollars per Annum.	Dollars per Week.
Minimum of existence .. .. : :	1,100–1,400	21 –27
Minimum for health and decency .. : :	1,500–1,800	28 –34½
Minimum for comfort .. .. : :	2,000–2,400	38½–46

(*Wages and the Family*, Chicago, 1925.)

An examination of Trade Union rates and other statistics of wages in important industries in the United States shows that, while many groups of skilled workers receive wages equal to or above Mr. Ogburn's minimum of comfort of about $38½ per week, many categories of unskilled workers receive wages considerably below his subsistence level of $30 per week.[1] At the beginning of 1926 the average actual earnings of male workers, without distinction according to skill or age, in representative industries in New York State, Illinois, and Massachusetts were about $28 to $32 per week. More comprehensive are the National Industrial Conference Board's statistics of actual earnings, which cover nearly three-quarters of a million workers in twenty-five important industries in different parts of the country.[2] They show the following averages for male workers in the first quarter of 1926 :—

	Average Weekly Earnings. Dollars.
Skilled	31·55
Unskilled	24·21
Weighted average	29·92

[1] Trade Union rates and also full-time weekly earnings in various occupations are published in the *Monthly Labor Review*.

[2] National Industrial Conference Board, *Wages in the United States*, New York, 1926.

Australia.

In this country, where attempts to apply the principles of the living wage have been the greatest, there are three standards to which reference is frequently made. The first is the Harvester Wage of 7s. a day, declared by Mr. Justice Higgins in the year 1907. This wage, which was considered a practicable minimum adequate for an unskilled labourer with a family (about five persons in all), was determined roughly without serious enquiry into the cost of living. Certain investigations were made, but the wage was, in fact, based largely on the rates paid by various municipal authorities to their unskilled workers. Nevertheless, this Harvester Wage, brought into conformity with the cost of living, i.e. the so-called Harvester equivalent, gradually became the basis of the Commonwealth Arbitration Court's decisions, and these, in their turn, exercised a considerable influence on the policy and awards of the wage tribunals in different States. The Harvester equivalents at various dates were approximately :—

			£	s.	d.	
Fourth quarter, 1914	..	..	2	14	7	per week
Fourth quarter, 1920	..	..	4	8	0	,,
First quarter, 1926	..	..	3	18	0	,,

The second Australian cost of living standard, which differs little from the Harvester standard, is that of the New South Wales Industrial Commission. The Commission is bound by law to declare at regular intervals the cost of living of a man, wife, and two children, and also that of an adult female. The amounts fixed become the minimum wages of adult male and female employees respectively. According to declarations dated December 15th, 1920, and August 24th, 1925, the amounts for adult male workers throughout the greater part of the State were :—

			£	s.	d.	
December 15th, 1920	..	..	4	5	0	per week
August 24th, 1925 ..	..	..	4	4	0	,, [1]

The third standard is that established by the Royal Commission appointed in 1919 to enquire into the cost of living according to reasonable standards of comfort for a family of five persons.[2] During the enquiry the Commission examined in great detail the cost of living in the capitals of the six States of the Commonwealth, about 450 family budgets being obtained, 800 witnesses heard, and a large number of price lists utilised. In its report the Commission gave a commodity budget according to Australian standards, very similar to the United States budget compiled under the direction of Dr. Meeker, to which reference has already been made. The average cost of the budget at the

[1] The *New South Wales Industrial Gazette*, August 1925. Other amounts had been declared at intervening dates. On August 24th, 1925, the weekly wage of adult female workers was declared to be £2 2s. 6d.

[2] The Commission consisted of three employers' representatives, three workers' representatives, and an impartial chairman, Mr. A. B. Piddington.

level of prices in November 1920, and the equivalent
cost during the first quarter of 1926, were :—

		£	s.	d.	
November 1920	.. .. ..	5	15	8	per week [1]
First quarter, 1926	.. ..	5	0	0	,,

The Commission merely reported on the cost of a
reasonable standard of comfort ; it had no power to
fix wages at the level required to enable that standard
to be attained, although it was generally thought that
wages would be fixed in accordance with its findings.
The amounts determined by the Commission were,
however, considerably higher than the minima in force,
and were also higher than the actual levels of wages
paid.   In November 1920 the Harvester equivalent
was about £4 8s. 0d. per week, while at about the same
date the average weekly wage rate, based on data for
skilled as well as for unskilled workers in the most
important industries of the Commonwealth, was
£4 9s. 10d. per week.   The practical impossibility of
fixing minimum wages for all adult male workers
without distinction at the level determined by the
Commission soon became evident.   Further reference
to this question is made in the following section.
Here it may suffice to repeat that in Australia at
least three different figures have been put forward,
each purporting to represent the necessary cost of

[1] Reports of the Royal Commission on the Basic Wage ;
see also *The Next Step : a Family Basic Income,* by Mr. Piddington.   The figure of £5 15s. 8d. is an average for the six capitals
of the Commonwealth.   The figures for the different cities
vary according to the cost of living.

living—namely, the Harvester equivalent, the New South Wales basic wage, and the Basic Wage Commission's estimate. The amounts necessary according to these standards at the level of prices during the fourth quarter of 1920 and the first quarter of 1926 were :—

Standard.	Amount per Week.	
	4th Quarter, 1920.	1st Quarter, 1926.
	£ s. d.	£ s. d.
Harvester equivalent	4 8 0	3 18 0
New South Wales basic wage [1] ..	4 5 0	4 4 0
Basic Wage Commission's estimate	5 15 8	5 0 0

The foregoing shows that considerable variations exist in estimates of the cost of living in Great Britain, the United States, and Australia. However, although in each country different estimates have been made of the sums considered necessary to maintain a family of given size, the differences are due largely to variations in the standards adopted. The poverty level can be distinguished clearly from the human needs standard, and this from a standard of comfort. Authorities will differ somewhat regarding the amount required for any one of these standards, but where a definite standard is specified, the variations in estimates are likely to be comparatively small.

[1] For a family of four persons ; the other figures are for a family of five. The New South Wales figure for 1926 is the declared basic wage ; the other 1926 figures are equivalents calculated by using cost of living index numbers.

THE LIVING WAGE IN RELATION TO THE WEALTH OF THE COMMUNITY.

In the preceding section it was shown that, within any country, widely differing estimates may be made of the cost of living of a family of given size. Some investigators, actuated by ethical considerations, endeavour to determine a wage which they consider desirable without paying much regard to what is practicable. Others give greater attention to what they believe to be attainable as a minimum in the early future.

In Australia, when the practicability of fixing wages to guarantee the standard proposed by the Basic Wage Commission was under consideration, the Commonwealth statistician, Mr. G. H. Knibbs, in a memorandum to the Prime Minister, stated that "such a wage cannot be paid to all adult employees because the whole produced wealth of the country, including all that portion of produced wealth which now goes in the shape of profit to employers, would not, if divided up equally amongst employees, yield the necessary weekly amount." In this case the Basic Wage Commission, when considering the items to be included in the budget, had gone beyond what was practicable for adoption as the minimum or basic wage for all adult male employees.[1]

[1] To meet the difficulty Mr. Piddington proposed that instead of paying a minimum wage of £5 15s. 8d. to all adult male workers, this amount should be received only by workers with wife and three children, and that larger or smaller

Whether the object be to indicate a standard of comfort considered desirable, or to determine a subsistence standard which is practically attainable, account must always be taken, directly or indirectly, of the actual standards of living of the community. These standards depend mainly on the wealth or productivity of the community. In consequence, standards of living are relative in character, and vary in the same community from one period to another, and in different communities at the same date. As progress is made in the industrial organisation and productive methods of any community, the standards will be raised. The standards are higher in wealthier than in poorer countries.[1] In those countries in which the living wage principle has been adopted, reference to the standard of the country is always expressed or

families should receive larger or smaller amounts. It was claimed that in this way the standard proposed by the Commission could be secured.

[1] The relative character of the living wage is clearly expressed by Mr. Justice Brown, of the South Australian Industrial Court in 1916 in the Plumbers' Case, as follows : " The statutory definition of the living wage is a wage adequate to meet the normal and reasonable needs of the worker. In other words, the conception is ethical rather than economic. The Court has not to determine the value of the services rendered, but to determine what is necessary to meet normal and reasonable needs. It should be obvious that in the interpretation of reasonable needs the Court cannot be wholly indifferent to the national income. The reasonable needs of the worker in a community where the national income is high are greater than the reasonable needs of the worker where the national income is low " (*South Australian Industrial Reports,* vol. I, 1916–18, p. 122).

implied. Thus in America wages are to be adequate according to American standards; in Australia, according to Australian standards, and so on.

To show relativity of standards from one country to another it may be of interest to compare the British, United States, and Australian standards for a family of five persons given in the preceding section. The table opposite gives these standards at the levels of prices at the beginning of 1926 in the currency of each country, and also in terms of the British currency unit, allowance being made for differences in the purchasing power of money in the different countries.[1] The standards are classified somewhat arbitrarily into three groups.

[1] The figures in British currency have been obtained by converting the American and Australian standards into terms of the level of prices in 1914 by using the ratios of the costs of living in 1914 and the beginning of 1926 in the United States (1914 = 100, 1926 = 176), and in Australia (1914 = 100, 1926 = 144). The 1914 equivalents have then been converted into British equivalents, account being taken not only of the rates of exchange, but also of differences between the purchasing power of money in the three countries. According to data obtained before the war by the Labour Department of the British Board of Trade, and by the South African Economic Commission, the ratios of the cost of living based on food and rent were : Great Britain 100, United States 152, Australia 124·5. Hence the cost of a given standard in the United States has been reduced in the ratio 152 : 100 to give its equivalent in Great Britain. Similarly the Australian costs have been reduced in the ratio 124·5 : 100. The equivalents in 1914 in Great Britain were then increased in the ratio 100 : 175, this representing the relation between the cost of living in Great Britain in 1914 and in March 1926.

Standard.	British.			United States.	Australian.		
	In Currency of Country.						
	£	s.	d.	$	£	s.	d.
Poverty	2	5	6	20	—		
Human needs ..	3	1	8	30	3	18	0[1]
Comfort	—			38½	5	0	0[2]
	In British Currency.						
Poverty	2	5	6	2 13 9	—		
Human needs ..	3	1	8	4 0 8	3	16	0[3]
Comfort	—			5 3 5	4	17	6[3]

By comparing the standards in British currency it is seen that the United States standards are higher than the Australian, and the Australian than the British. Evidently these levels are influenced largely by prevailing standards of living within each country, which, in turn, depend on the *per capita* wealth of the community.

PRINCIPLES BASED ON THE LIVING WAGE.

Although the living wage is not capable of exact expression, it may be of considerable practical value if taken in relation to the productivity of the community. It is possible to determine in any community the minimum below which no workers should fall. This minimum should be considered apart from the

[1] Harvester equivalent at the beginning of 1926.

[2] Basic Wage Commission equivalent at the beginning of 1926.

[3] The differences between these figures and those given in the currency of the country are due to the higher purchasing power of the pound in Great Britain than in Australia.

conditions of any given establishment or industry. It is the distinctive feature of the living wage principle that, at the basis of the wage system, there should be a minimum determined by the general productivity of the community as a whole, without taking account of the prosperity of individual establishments or industries. This feature is recognised in numerous basic wage decisions in Australia. For example, in 1909, Mr. Justice Higgins, President of the Commonwealth Arbitration Court, expressed the view that " it is necessary to keep this living wage a thing sacrosanct, beyond the reach of bargaining," and added that if a man be unable to maintain his enterprise without cutting down the wages essential for his workers, it would be better that he should abandon the enterprise.

It follows that where there are differences in the cost of living in different districts, there should be corresponding differences in money wages. If a change takes place in the purchasing power of money in any community without a change in the general productivity of goods and services, then the minimum wage should be adjusted to such changes by means of a sliding scale. This is necessary in order to ensure the maintenance of the minimum real wage. If there is a change in national productivity, or in the forces determining the workers' share of the national income, a change in minimum wages is justifiable.

Finally, if the living wage idea be accepted, special consideration is necessary in the case of workers whose earnings may be reduced owing to the casual or seasonal character of their employment. For such workers a minimum hourly or daily wage, higher than that of workers whose employment is regular, is essential if their standard of living is not to fall below the general minimum. Similarly, with the object of preventing the standard of living of piece-workers from falling below that of workers in regular employment on a minimum time wage, piece rates should be such that under ordinary circumstances workers of average ability would be able to earn an amount at least equal to the minimum time rate. If, through no fault of their own, e.g. a break-down of machinery, their earnings fall below the minimum time wage, they should be guaranteed this minimum.

CHAPTER V

CAPACITY OF INDUSTRY TO PAY

THE productivity of industry is the source from which wages are paid, and no legislative process or manipulation by State-established machinery can raise wages above the level that industry can bear. Even where the necessity of taking into account the productivity of industry is not expressly stated in minimum wage laws which endorse the living wage principle, in their application account is taken directly or indirectly of the capacity of industry to pay.

The present chapter attempts to show that the principal solution of wage problems lies in increased productivity, that wages in any individual establishment or industry should not depend on the capacity of each to pay without reference to the wages which other establishments or industries can afford, and that the level of minimum wages should be based on the capacity of industry *in general* to pay.

IMPORTANCE OF INCREASING PRODUCTIVITY.

The wages of the lowest paid groups of workers may be increased either by a change in distribution or by an increase in the total productivity of the community. Social justice may demand changes in distribution in consequence of the existence, side by side, of extremes of wealth and poverty. A change in distribution may be at the expense of other groups of workers, or of other classes of the community. There is, however, little likelihood of considerable increases in minimum wages by measures of redistribution. The amounts which skilled workers receive are generally no more than a reasonable return for the training they have undergone, and for their higher efficiency. As regards other classes of the community, the number of persons receiving large incomes is small if compared with the total number of workers, and to transfer the greater part of those incomes to the workers would add little to the wage which each receives.[1]

Dr. A. L. Bowley's study of the division of the product of industry before the war between different classes of the community is a sufficient warning to those who hope that considerable increases in the wages of a large part of the working population are practicable by the transfer to the workers of a portion of the national income now going to other classes of the community.[2] On the basis of data for 1907 it is shown that if, at that date, one-half of profits had been transferred to the wage-earners, average wages would have been raised by about 21 per cent., or to about the level of Mr. Rowntree's minimum of 35s. 3d.

---

[1] The fact that redistribution would add little to the wage of each worker does not invalidate the case for redistribution where necessary to secure social justice.

[2] *The Division of the Product of Industry : an Analysis of National Income before the War*, by Dr. A. L. Bowley, Oxford, 1919.

per week.[1] This minimum could only be reached by
all workers if at the same time the earnings of skilled
workers had been reduced to that level. Dr. Bowley
adds that " the raising of wages, whether by a legally
enforced minimum or otherwise, might force employers
to become more efficient, or if a small number of
inefficient employers were obliged to stop, others might
be able to extend their operations so as to give the
same aggregate employment ; evidently this progress
cannot go very far without radical changes in
methods." [2] He points out that, although an effective
demand for higher wages would tend to a better and
more economical use of capital, skill of management
is limited, and the best results cannot be universally
obtained.

Similar conclusions as to the inadequacy of the
national dividend to ensure considerable increases in
wages by measures of redistribution have been reached
by Sir Josiah Stamp. In 1920 he made a calculation showing that if all people with incomes over
£250 per annum were to pool the excess over that
amount, and if from the pool thus formed a sum were
withdrawn equal to the amounts obtained by taxation
to support the national services and savings for capital
extensions on the pre-war scale, the remainder would
provide not more than 5s. per week per family. This

[1] This included women as well as men. According to
information given in Dr. Bowley's study, *The Change in the
Distribution of the National Income, 1880–1913*, the average of
all incomes in the United Kingdom in 1913 was £104 per annum.

[2] *The Division of the Product of Industry*, p. 41.

calculation was made again in 1925, when it was found that the remainder for distribution would have been almost certainly between £25,000,000 and £100,000,000, which sum was not enough to provide 5s. per week per family. [1]

An examination made by Dr. Bowley of changes in the distribution of the National Income between 1880 and 1913 shows a high degree of constancy of many of the proportions of the national income going to different classes, and suggests that little change in distribution is practicable.[2] A somewhat similar situation has been shown to exist in the United States. Dr. W. I. King has made calculations on the basis of the United States census statistics showing that there is little variation over a period of years in the percentage of " value added by manufacture " paid in wages.[3] The figures covering all manufacturing industries are :—

				Per cent;
1889	..	..	..	.. 44
1899	..	..	..	.. 42
1904	..	..	..	.. 41
1909	..	..	..	.. 40
1914	..	..	..	.. 41
1919	..	..	..	.. 42

[1] *Wealth and Taxable Capacity*, p. 96 ; *The Times*, August 3rd, 1925, p. 10, account of an address by Sir Josiah Stamp at the Liberal Summer School, Cambridge.

[2] *The Change in the Distribution of the National Income, 1880-1913*, by Dr. A. L. Bowley, see p. 26.

[3] These data were published in the *New York Evening Post*, June 7th, 1922. See also a paper read by Mr. George Soule before the 35th Annual Meeting of the American Economic Association, Chicago, December 1922, published in the supplement to the *American Economic Review*, March 1923, p. 136.

E

In considering the adequacy of different rates of wages, American writers have in mind higher minimum standards of living than those generally advocated in European countries. It is claimed that, according to American standards, the wages of many groups of workers are deplorably low, that, even if complete justice in distribution were assured, the total product is not sufficient for any great increase in the *per capita* wage, and that the main hope lies in an increase in productivity.[1]

CAPACITY TO PAY OF INDIVIDUAL ESTABLISHMENTS OR INDUSTRIES.

The conclusions of the preceding section, which are probably true for almost all countries, should not be regarded as destroying in any way the value of minimum wage legislation. The principal means of raising wages is an increase in the total volume available for distribution together with a restriction

[1] See Professor W. C. Mitchell's estimate of income of the United States and E. M. Patterson's article on " Factors determining Real Wages," published in the *Annals of the American Academy of Political Science*, March 1922. Professor Paul H. Douglas in *Wages and the Family*, after reaching similar conclusions as to the inadequacy of the present rates of wages in the United States, proposes the family allowance system as a solution. As regards Great Britain, Mr. Rowntree, in discussing various methods of increasing wages, says that an increase in the productivity of industry, whether due to better organisation and machinery, greater efficiency on the part of the workers or management, or any other factor, is the most important means (*The Human Needs of Labour*, p. 137).

of the number and an improvement in the quality of the population. Nevertheless, the prevention of sweating and of the continued existence of a number of wage-earners at standards seriously below those of the remainder of the community is the urgent necessity of a progressive State.

The existence of sweated labour is partly the result of the uncontrolled application of the principle of paying wages according to the capacity to pay of each individual establishment or industry. Employers in industries which depend on low-paid labour claim that they cannot pay as high wages as employers in other industries. Also employers assert that because the profitableness of their establishments is lower than that of the rest of the industry, their wages should be fixed at a lower level. In a number of cases employers have demanded that the minimum wage for their industry should be based on that paid to the lowest class of worker in the district in which the cost of living is lowest. Where these claims are accepted, not only may the standard of living of various groups of workers fall considerably below the general level, but wage rates are not in any degree standardised.[1] This is the situation in most countries at the present time, except in so far as standardisation of wages has

[1] It might be expected that marked inequalities could be of a temporary character only, owing to the tendency of workers to move from low-paid industries and districts to those in which wages are high. This tendency, however, operates very slowly owing to difficulties in the way of full mobility of labour.

been effected by collective agreements. It is precisely, however, in industries in which organisation is not adequate to secure the advantages of collective agreements that a low standard of living and a high degree of lack of uniformity of wage rates are generally found. Also it is not enough to secure what Professor Pigou has called an economic wage, i.e. a wage which, " in the conditions of the trade under review, economic forces tend to bring about if employers can be prevented from taking advantage of the bargaining weakness of some, or all, of their workpeople, and paying them less than they are worth." [1] Some limitation of the system of allowing each industry or establishment to pay wages based on its own financial condition is necessary.

Capacity to Pay of Industry in General.

In view of the relation between wages and productivity, and also of the desirability of fixing minimum wages so as to prevent the continued existence of sweated labour, the best basis for minimum wages appears to be the capacity of industry in general.[2]

---

[1] *Economic Journal*, September 1922, article on " Trade Boards and the Cave Committee," p. 318.

[2] How much industry in general can bear is evidently difficult of measurement, while potential capacity is still more problematic. Often, at present, there is great difficulty in obtaining the facts, and one of the essentials of the future is more complete knowledge of the profits of industry. Much industrial unrest, and the loss which this entails, would be avoided if those responsible for the financial side of production

This conclusion is in agreement with that reached in the chapter on the living wage, namely, that at the basis of the wage system there should be a minimum wage determined by the general productivity of the community as a whole without taking account of the prosperity of individual establishments or industries.

It would be impracticable to fix wages at the *average* level which industry in general pays, as this would be beyond the capacity of a large part of industry, including many trades so important to the economic life of the nation that they must be safeguarded against injury. It should, however, be possible, on the basis of the capacity of industry in general, to fix a minimum which, while not hampering the important industries, would prevent the payment of unduly low wages. As a consequence of this a number of the least efficient workers might lose their employment, certain inefficient employers be forced out of business, and a few sweated industries of minor importance be eliminated. These consequences may well be lesser evils than the perpetuation of inefficiency and misery which follow the payment of a wage unreasonably low in relation to national productivity.[1]

would take the workers and the public more into their confidence. This gaining of confidence will be facilitated as the necessity for a rate of interest high enough to call forth a sufficient supply of capital and to ensure adequate saving is more generally recognised. See *The Facts of Industry, the Case for Publicity*, Macmillan & Co., 1926.

[1] Industries or establishments paying such wages are in many cases parasitic, since either the workers are partly maintained by the earnings of other workers, e.g. where

The fixing of minimum wages in relation to the capacity to pay of industry in general has already received some application in practice. In giving effect to certain minimum wage laws the principle has been established that it is no part of the duty of the wage-fixing body to ensure profits to *all* employers in an industry, or to protect those who are inefficient. Nor is it obliged to allow unduly low wages in industries or establishments which are in difficulties owing to natural handicaps, e.g. where a mine is nearing exhaustion, or is faced with the competition of mines with much richer deposits.[1] In Australasia especially the view is generally accepted that if an industry or establishment cannot pay what is considered a reasonable minimum, it had better cease to exist, and its workers transfer to some other industry. The principle that the wages of the worker should not depend on the profits made by the individual employer is well expressed in the decision of the Australian Commonwealth Arbitration Court in 1909 in the case of the Broken Hill Proprietary Company, as follows :—

" First of all, is an employer who is poor to be ordered to pay as high wages as an employer who is rich ? Now without laying down a rule absolute and

women workers receiving very low wages are in part supported by their husbands, or, if supporting themselves, have not enough for health and efficiency, and the consequences involve a charge on society for hospitals and charitable institutions.

[1] In such cases the employer has to pay the same price as his rivals for the raw materials he buys, and similarly it is reasonable that he should be subject to the same minimum wage.

unconditional under all circumstances, I strongly hold the view that, unless the circumstances are very exceptional, the needy employer should, under an award, pay at the same rate as his richer rival. It would not otherwise be possible to prevent the sweating of employees, the growth of parasitic industries, the spread of industrial unrest—unrest which it is the function of this Court to allay. If a man cannot maintain his enterprise without cutting down the wages which are proper to be paid to his employees—at all events the wages which are essential for their living—it would be better that he should abandon the enterprise." [1]

STANDARDS OF SKILLED WORKERS.

There is an essential difference between the minimum or basic wage below which no worker should be allowed to fall and higher wages paid to skilled workers. The case is strong for fixing the basic wage as a means of preventing misery, and State regulation may easily be justified. With regard to wages above the basic

[1] *Commonwealth Arbitration Reports*, vol. III, 1909. Similar decisions have been reached in the awards of various State Arbitration Courts, e.g. in South Australia and Western Australia. Thus, in the decision of the South Australian Industrial Court in the Furniture Trades Case, 1918, it is indicated that it may be better for the Court to fix wages on general principles than to attempt to preserve in the State every factory that may chance to have established itself. The extinction of industries unsuited to the State may be an advantage rather than to allow a long and fruitless struggle under severe competition to continue. (*South Australian Industrial Reports*, vol. II, 1918–19.)

minimum, compulsory regulation is less urgent, as the economic conditions of the workers are better. However, in certain cases, skilled workers are unable to secure the satisfactory regulation of their wages by means of collective agreements. Also it is often convenient to use machinery set up with the object of preventing sweating to fix the wage rates of skilled as well as of unskilled workers in the trades concerned. Finally, Arbitration Courts, in making awards for the purpose of maintaining industrial peace, frequently fix the rates of wages of skilled as well as of unskilled workers.

Where minimum wages are fixed for skilled workers, the basis is often different from that adopted for unskilled workers. Thus in Australasia, although frequently the capacity to pay of individual establishments and industries is not taken into consideration in fixing the basic wages of unskilled workers, the prosperity of individual industries is usually a factor of importance in fixing the wage rates of other categories of workers. For these rates, however, little or no account is taken of the position of individual employers. To do so would be undesirable as the standardisation of wages would be prevented, and unfair competition between different employers would result.

CONSEQUENCES OF FIXING A MINIMUM WAGE.

In determining, at any time, the minimum below which no worker should be allowed to fall, the practical problems to consider are the reactions on employers, workers, and the community as a whole.

Employers.

State machinery may establish a minimum wage, but employers are not obliged to engage workers at that wage, their only obligation being that if they employ workers, they shall pay at least the rate fixed. If, therefore, a minimum wage is fixed, some employers may find their costs of production increased. This will be the case if the increase in wages does not lead to a corresponding increase in the efficiency of the workers, or stimulate employers to introduce improved methods of manufacture. A rise in costs of production implies a loss of markets which will be greater or less according as demand for the commodities produced is elastic or not.[1] Loss of markets will be followed by a reduction in the scale of production, or even a closing down of plant.

The elimination of establishments or industries which are unable to exist except by sweated labour may be considered desirable. Left to themselves certain establishments may continue for a long time to struggle with antiquated methods and machinery in competition with factories highly organised and fitted with the latest appliances. They cannot pay

[1] Demand is elastic if a small increase (or decrease) in price is followed by a considerable reduction (or increase) in demand. In the case of an inelastic demand the converse is true, namely, that small increases or decreases in price have little effect on the quantities purchased.

good wages, and yet the workers, from custom, ignorance, or lack of mobility, remain with them.[1] The fixing of a reasonable minimum wage would shorten the struggle, and the workers would turn earlier to establishments employing more productive methods.   Also certain industries may be ill-adapted to a given country, and may be subjected to the competition of foreign producers with superior natural advantages.   It is preferable that the capital and labour they employ should be diverted, without delay, to other industries more suited to the country than that the misery of a protracted struggle should be endured.

Workers.

If wages are fixed at too high a level, unemployment will result.   In other words, demand for labour at that level is less than supply.   The question, therefore, is largely one of choice between a higher level of wages with a larger volume of unemployment or a lower level of wages with less unemployment.   Where unemployment results, those thrown out of work will in some cases be absorbed into new or growing industries.   In other cases, however, they will compete for employment on the labour market, and in consequence there may be a slight reduction in the general level of wages.   To the extent to which this is true, the

---

[1] The case of hand-loom weavers in the early nineteenth century may be cited as an example of the misery which attends unequal struggles between antiquated and improved methods.

cost of the prevention of sweating is distributed over the general body of wage-earners.

The Community as a Whole.

Where demand for the products of an industry is inelastic a rise in wages will be covered by an increase in the price of the commodities produced, and there will be little or no falling off in demand for the product of the industry concerned. Thus unemployment will not be caused in that industry, and the cost of the improvement in wages will be borne by the community as a whole through the higher price which it will pay for the products of the industry.[1] An increase in the prices of commodities hitherto produced under sweated conditions is easily justifiable, as the community had been unconsciously undervaluing the labour involved.[2] The immediate cause of the low wages was largely competition between employers, and the harmful effects on the workers are diminished or avoided if wages are standardised at a higher level by means of minimum wage machinery.

Where the demand for products is elastic a rise in wages, followed by an increase in price, will cause unemployment in the industry concerned. Since, however, there are some wages so low as to imply a degree of misery which the State should not permit,

[1] This will reduce the purchasing power available for other goods, and may cause unemployment or a slight fall in wages in the trades producing them.

[2] See *The Living Wage* by H. N. Brailsford, J. A. Hobson, A. Creech Jones, and E. F. Wise, London, 1926, pp. 28–9.

it may be a gain rather than a loss to prohibit the employment of workers for totally inadequate remuneration.   Provision for those thrown out of work, either by means of unemployment insurance benefits or by direct maintenance by the State, is logically inevitable.   It should be recognised that, in paying benefits to those who thus lose their employment until they obtain work elsewhere, the State is incurring a charge rather than permit certain of its members to be employed at wages considerably below the level which the income of the community can sustain.   In other words, a contribution is made by the remainder of the community for the prevention of extreme poverty.   Maintenance by the State will be permanent in the case of those unemployable at the rates fixed.[1] At the same time, in order that the number of the unemployable may be reduced to a minimum, special facilities for finding employment in other occupations should be provided.   Similarly, training centres for teaching new trades are of value.

---

[1] In Fabian Tract No. 128, *The Case for a Legal Minimum Wage*, page 12, the view is expressed that "it is far cheaper for the nation to deal with the unemployable as destitute persons by wisely adapted poor law methods than to allow them to drag down decent workers to their level by their competition in the labour market."   This is true in some cases, while in others, special permits may be issued to enable certain workers to work for wages below the minimum.   The issue of such permits might be accompanied by the provision of State aid to prevent the standard falling below the minimum fixed.   The question of the issue of permits is dealt with in a later chapter.

DEDUCTIONS.

The general level of wages depends on total productivity, and the principal means of increasing wages is not by fundamental changes in distribution, but by increasing productivity. An increase in general productivity will almost certainly lead to an increase in the wages of the lowest paid groups of workers.

The capacity to pay of industry in general, rather than the wages which individual establishments or industries can afford, should be taken as basis for a minimum wage of general application.

At any time the basic minimum wage must be within the reach of the great majority of undertakings in all important industries, but by the continued operation of minimum wage machinery it should be possible to raise the minimum progressively until it is effective for a considerable proportion of unskilled workers.

CHAPTER VI

A NATIONAL MINIMUM

THE conclusions reached in the two preceding chapters point to the desirability of a national minimum wage based on national productivity. There is no conflict between the living wage defined in relation to national productivity and the wage which industry in general can pay. In fact, the two conceptions are practically identical, and each leads to a national, or in some cases a regional, basis for fixing minimum wages below which no worker of ordinary ability should fall. Both national productivity and the capacity of industry in general to pay are, however, difficult of determination. The statistics necessary are not available ; therefore some indirect method must be adopted provisionally.

In the present chapter wage statistics are considered as throwing light on what industry can bear, thus furnishing a means to determining a practicable minimum. Also the problems are discussed of fixing minimum wages in districts in which the cost of living is unequal, of allowing for changes in the purchasing power of money from one period to another, and of taking into account changes in the capacity of industry.

METHOD OF DETERMINING THE MINIMUM.

Adequate information not being available as to the capacity of industry in general to pay, the best alternative is to secure statistics with regard to prevailing standards of living. Among the data suitable for this purpose are the results of wage censuses.[1] These show what industry in general is actually paying. They also show the relative levels of wages in different industries and districts, and thus enable attention to be directed particularly to cases where conditions are considerably below the generally prevailing standard. Thus the British Wage Census of 1907, by revealing very low wages in certain industries, contributed largely to the adoption of the minimum wage legislation of 1909.

For the purpose of determining a practicable minimum below which wages should not be allowed to fall, information with regard to the wages of unskilled workers in different industries may be taken as guide. By means of a wage census, statistics can be obtained as to the earnings of unskilled adult male and female workers in different industries. The earnings of such workers in the large or well-organised industries may be regarded as standard of comparison. It would evidently be unsatisfactory, however, to take the *average* wage of unskilled workers in the well-organised industries as the minimum wage. In the well-organised industries themselves the wages of unskilled workers differ considerably from one industry to another, while within each industry wages may vary in the

[1] Family budget enquiries also provide valuable information as to family income and the distribution of expenditure on the different items entering into the cost of living.

different establishments. The figures given below illustrate the range from one industry to another in the full-time weekly wages of unskilled male workers in Great Britain and Germany, and the average hourly earnings of unskilled male workers in the United States.[1] The number of hours in a full-time week vary somewhat from one industry to another, but the variation is only to a small extent the cause of differences in the wages in different industries. In Great Britain the range in wages is abnormally great owing to the fact that industries which have felt the pressure of foreign competition have sustained much heavier reductions of wages during the depression which began in 1921 than the so-called "sheltered industries."

GREAT BRITAIN.

Weekly Rates of Unskilled Workers at September 30th, 1925.

	s.	d.
Building	55	7
Engineering	40	2
Shipbuilding	38	5
Railways	46	0 [2]
Local authorities	53	5
Gas works	52	11
Electrical supply	54	10

[1] The British figures are taken from the *Ministry of Labour Gazette*, October 1925. The figures for Germany are from *Wirtschaft und Statistik*, No. 18, September 1925. Both the British and German figures are averages based on data for the chief towns or principal centres. The United States figures are compiled by the National Industrial Conference Board, an employers' association. They are based on statistics of earnings obtained from the pay-rolls of a large number of representative firms.

[2] Certain classes of porters only.

GERMANY.

Weekly Rates of Unskilled Workers in August 1925.

					R.Mks.
Building	..	..	..	..	44·37
Mining	..	..	..	..	32·58
Metal	..	..	..	..	30·31
Chemical	..	..	..	..	32·54
Wood	..	..	..	..	39·75
Paper	..	..	..	..	28·66
Textiles	..	..	..	..	24·67
Brewing	..	..	..	..	40·47
Printing	..	..	..	..	40·16
National railways		..	..	..	32·29
Weighted average [1]			..	..	32·85

UNITED STATES.

Average Hourly Earnings of Unskilled Workers in July 1925.

					Cents.
Iron and steel	..	..	..	..	49·8
Foundries ..	..	..	..	..	50·7
Automobiles	..	..	..	..	50·9
Chemicals ..	..	..	..	..	49·2
Furniture ..	..	..	..	..	42·3
Meat packing	..	..	..	..	46·2
Wool	..	..	..	..	50·0
Paper and pulp	..	..	..	..	45·2
Boot and shoe	..	..	..	..	39·8
Lumber and mill work	..	..	..	36·7
Average [1]		..	..	..	47·0

The wage paid to unskilled workers in the lowest
paid industry in which employers and workers are
well organised might be taken as minimum wage for a
district or country. Any one industry is, however,
unsatisfactory as basis owing to the effects on it of

---

[1] Including other industrial groups.

F

exceptional economic conditions. The minimum wage
should be established on a broader basis. Although
suffering from the defect of being arbitrary, perhaps
the most satisfactory method would be to fix the
minimum at a given proportion of the average wage
paid to unskilled workers in well-organised industries.
Thus the minimum wage might be fixed at, say,
80 per cent. of the average wage paid to unskilled
workers in certain of the chief industries of the district
or country.[1]

In selecting the industries to be taken as basis, it
would be desirable to omit those in which wages are
abnormally high or low owing to their special character.
Thus, for example, in most countries wages for a full
working week in the building industry are higher than
those in most other industries, largely to make up for
irregularity of employment. Again, at any given date
wages in certain industries may be exceptionally low
or high owing to special conditions of a temporary
character. In the figures given above for Great
Britain, wages in the engineering and shipbuilding
industries are abnormally low in relation to those paid
in other industries. In order to avoid the effects of
temporary features account should as far as possible
be taken of wages over a sufficiently long period with
reasonably stable conditions.

---

[1] This would be, in effect, to fix the minimum in relation
to the wages of other groups of workers. The relation between
this basis and those of the living wage and the capacity of
industry to pay was noted in Chapter III.

VARIATIONS IN THE COST OF LIVING ACCORDING TO DISTRICT.

Statistical enquiries show appreciable differences in the cost of living from one district to another within any country, although requirements of food, clothing, housing accommodation, fuel, light, and other commodities are similar for the same grade of worker. In fixing minimum wages the object should be to secure equality of *real* wages in different parts of the country. This implies variation in *money* wages according to differences in the cost of living.

In order to attain equality of real wages the wage-fixing authority may establish not a money minimum but a real minimum consisting of quantities of various articles of food, clothing, fuel and light, housing accommodation, and other commodities.[1] The total cost of these in any district would be taken as the money minimum wage for that district. A variant of this method is to determine the minimum money wage for a given district and then to fix money wages in other districts in accordance with the relative cost of living so as to equalise real wages in all districts. This

[1] These quantities can be established on the results of family budget enquiries. Such enquiries have been conducted at various dates in a number of countries. The International Conference of Labour Statisticians held in Geneva in April 1925 passed a resolution recommending that those countries which had made no recent family budget enquiries should undertake such investigations as soon as conditions are sufficiently stable. Methods of conducting family budget enquiries are discussed in the International Labour Office Study, No. 9, Series N (Statistics), Geneva, 1926.

method is exactly the same in principle as that of the sliding scale which has been so widely applied during and since the war for the purpose of maintaining equality of real wages during periods of changing prices.

The adjustment of wages in various localities in which the cost of living is different is not free from difficulties, the chief of which is the determination of the limits of each district. Statistics show that the cost of living often varies more according to size of town than according to geographical region, and this adds to the difficulty of defining the limits of the areas for which a given money wage shall be fixed.

In a later chapter an outline is given of the policy adopted by minimum wage fixing bodies in determining wages for similar categories of workers in different districts. It may be noted here, however, that in Great Britain the Trade Boards have generally adopted the system of fixing uniform money rates for a given category of workers in different districts.[1] This has led to complaints by employers in small towns that the rates fixed have been too high. Such complaints are justified if the cost of living is lower in the

[1] Various exceptions are indicated later. The difficulties under consideration are encountered not only by minimum wage fixing bodies, but also when collective agreements are being concluded by Trade Unions covering a whole country. In such cases localities are often graded, and wages differ by some recognised proportion from one grade of locality to another. This practice is common in Germany, and is also adopted in the building trade, railway, and other agreements in Great Britain.

small towns, as the fixing of a uniform money wage for small as for large towns implies that a higher real wage is being paid in the former. They are also justified if workers in the small towns are less efficient than those in large towns. Where the differences in the cost of living or in efficiency are not large, however, the British practice of fixing uniform rates of wages for similar categories of workers in the different districts is not unsatisfactory. It has the advantage that the difficult problem of classifying districts according to differences in the cost of living is avoided. Also if uniform rates are fixed there is a tendency for differences in the cost of living to disappear.[1] Further, the tendency of workers to move to the large towns to earn the higher wages paid there would, to a considerable extent, be overcome.

Index numbers showing differences in the cost of living from place to place would be of value as a guide in determining whether the inequalities are too great to permit of uniform money wages, and if so the adjustments necessary to secure the same real wages. In Great Britain recent information is not available showing the cost of living in different districts.[2] In a

[1] This tendency appears to have operated in a number of countries during the war owing partly to the regulation of prices and an increase in the mobility of goods, but no doubt partly also to the regulation of wages, greater uniformity of rates being established.

[2] Enquiries were made in 1905 and 1912 by the Board of Trade (*Cost of Living of the Working Classes*, Reports of Enquiries, Cd. 3864 of 1908, and Cd. 6955 of 1913) into rents, retail prices, and standard rates of wages in the principal towns

number of countries, however, such data are published regularly in connection with the monthly or quarterly cost of living statistics. The table opposite gives index numbers for various towns or districts in Germany, Sweden, Switzerland, Great Britain, Canada, and Australia, showing inequalities in the cost of living. In each country the cost of living in the first town or district is taken as base ($=100$) and that in each other town or locality expressed as a percentage. The index numbers are not comparable internationally. In Australia, statistics showing the relation between the cost of living in various districts are used by minimum wage fixing bodies for the purpose of adjusting money rates of wages in such a way as to secure equality of real wages in different localities.

CHANGES IN THE COST OF LIVING.

If the cost of living changes in any district a fixed money wage represents a higher or lower real wage

of the United Kingdom. Figures were compiled showing the relation of rents, retail prices, and standard rates of wages in certain occupations in various districts in comparison with those in London. The results of the two enquiries were generally very similar. The 1912 figures showed that retail prices in areas outside London were 97·4 per cent. of those in London ; rents in other towns were 58·4 per cent. of those in London, while rents and retail prices together outside London were 89·6 per cent. of those in London. Thus the chief cause of the differences was variations in rents, i.e. the most fixed and durable item entering into the cost of living, and these generally varied according to the size of the town. Outside London wages in the occupations covered were about 84 per cent. of the London level.

INDEX NUMBERS SHOWING LOCAL VARIATIONS IN THE COST
OF LIVING WITHIN CERTAIN COUNTRIES GENERALLY
DURING 1925 OR 1926.[1]

Country and Locality.	Index Numbers.	Country and Locality.	Index Numbers.
Germany—		*Great Britain* [2]*—*	
Berlin	100·0	London	100·0
Hamburg.. ..	106·8	Newcastle-on-Tyne	95·0
Coblenz	107·1	Liverpool ..	89·0
Lubeck	97·5	Manchester ..	88·0
Lüneburg ..	94·2	Birmingham ..	87·0
Magdeburg ..	88·6	Warrington ..	85·0
Sweden—		*Canada—*	
Stockholm ..	100·0	Ontario	100·0
Lulea	90·0	Nova Scotia ..	103·7
Upsala	85·8	Quebec	95·6
Kristianstad ..	80·8	Manitoba ..	99·8
Jönköping ..	75·3	Alberta	104·8
Visby	79·1	British Columbia	116·6
Switzerland—		*Australia—*	
Berne	100·0	Sydney	100·0
Lucerne	100·1	Melbourne ..	96·0
Schaffhausen ..	100·6	Adelaide.. ..	96·2
Bâle	100·6	Perth	94·0
Lausanne.. ..	102·4	Brisbane	85·7
Geneva	107·0	Hobart	95·5

[1] For Switzerland the index numbers are based on food
prices only, while for Sweden, fuel and light are also
included ; those for Australia cover food, groceries, and
housing ; those for Great Britain cover food, housing, and
coal, and those for Germany and Canada include food, fuel,
light, and housing. Similar indices are available for 1913–14
in the cases of Germany and Canada ; they show a considerably wider range than that indicated above.

[2] Figures for 1912.

according as prices have fallen or risen. Unless, however, there have been other changes than that in the cost of living, e.g. a change in productivity, the minimum real wage should be maintained unchanged. This is effected by adjusting the money minimum to changes in the cost of living by means of a sliding scale.

The sliding scale system has been so widely adopted since 1914 that it is unnecessary to describe it in detail here. It may suffice to emphasise a few points of a general character. The first is the importance of sound methods for the compilation of index numbers showing changes in the cost of living.[1] Then, according to some systems of adjustment, part of the wage is fixed and part varies with the cost of living. In order to maintain the real wage unchanged, however, it is necessary that the *whole* wage should be variable in proportion to changes in the cost of living. The system of adjustment should include a provision that the wage will be changed only if the cost of living varies by not less than a given proportion, e.g. 5 per cent. In this way minor fluctuations are avoided. The frequency with which wages should be adjusted depends on the rapidity with which prices change. If the price level is changing slowly, annual adjustments of wages may be adequate. In Germany even weekly

[1] On this question a number of resolutions were adopted at the Second International Conference of Labour Statisticians held in Geneva, April 1925. A report prepared for the Conference describes the methods adopted in various countries for the compilation of index numbers of the cost of living.

adjustments were not frequent enough to keep pace with the unparalleled depreciation of the value of the currency during the height of the inflationary period in 1923.

The cost of living sliding scale system is of value only for maintaining real wages at a given level during periods of changing prices. If there is an increase or decrease in productivity a corresponding change in real wages may be justified, but the rigid application of the cost of living sliding scale system would prevent such alterations. Thus if this system alone had been adopted at the beginning of the nineteenth century the workers would not have benefited from the great increases in production following the rapid developments of machinery which took place during the century. Improvements in productive processes leading to an increase in the supply of goods and a fall in prices would be followed, under the sliding scale system, by reductions in money wages, real wages remaining unchanged. Clearly such a situation would be unsatisfactory and, by reducing demand for commodities, would impose a serious check on increasing productivity. A method of avoiding this is now considered.

CHANGES IN THE CAPACITY OF INDUSTRY TO PAY.

The relation between the living wage and total productivity, and the interpretation of the principle of capacity to pay in terms of what industry in general can afford, imply that wages, including minimum wages, should vary with changes in total productivity. In other words, if productivity increases, real wages should increase, and vice versa.

To make such adjustments an index of changes in total productivity is necessary. Indices on the lines required have been constructed in certain countries, notably in the United States.[1] The method adopted is to use series of statistics showing year by year the quantities of different commodities produced, e.g. tons of coal, iron, steel, bushels of wheat. Series are selected which give the physical volume of the products of agriculture, mining, and manufacturing industries. The number of commodities included ranges from twenty to one hundred in different compilations.

It is then necessary to combine the separate data into a single series indicative of general changes in material production. In doing so allowance must be

---

[1] For the United States, mention may be made of the researches of Dr. W. I. King, Dr. W. W. Stewart (*American Economic Review*, March 1921), and Dr. E. E. Day (*Harvard Review of Economic Statistics*, January 1921, and subsequent numbers). Indices of production are also published by the United States Department of Commerce in its *Survey of Current Business*, and by the Federal Reserve Board in its *Bulletin*. An article on "Indexes of Productivity of Labor" was published in the *U.S. Monthly Labor Review*, July 1926.

In Australia the Commonwealth Statistician compiles statistics showing the value and volume of production. These are published in *Production Bulletins* and also in the *Commonwealth Year Book*. For Great Britain the studies made by Dr. Bowley into changes in the national income may be noted.

made for differences in the relative importance of the commodities included. Thus in Great Britain an increase of 50 per cent. in coal output would be far more important from the point of view of national productivity than a corresponding increase in the production of beet sugar. Allowance may be made by applying to the various series weights based on the relative importance of each commodity in the field of national production, e.g. the number of persons employed in the various industries.[1]

If an increase in total productivity is merely the result of an increase in the total number of persons engaged in production, then, other things being equal, real wages should remain unchanged. Therefore, in constructing an index of material production for the adjustment of wages, account must be taken of changes in population, or rather in the number of persons gainfully employed. This is done by reducing the statistics to a *per capita* basis.

Changes in material production are generally irregular from year to year. Although a sound policy of credit control may diminish the degree of irregularity, it is probable that for many years to come cyclical fluctuations of industrial activity will remain a feature of economic life. It is undesirable that the basic minimum wage should follow closely the ups and downs of productivity during the business cycle, but

[1] Weights showing relative importance may also be based on other criteria, e.g. the aggregate value of production of each commodity, or the value added in the process of production.

rather the steady trend of *per capita* production over a period of years. Instead, therefore, of adjusting the wage each year in proportion to productivity in that year as compared with productivity during the previous year, the system of the long-period moving average might be adopted. Annual adjustments on the basis of a ten-year moving average have been suggested in the United States. Such a system would avoid variations from year to year in consequence merely of cyclical booms and depressions. It might be supplemented by the proviso that only after an appreciable change in productivity should the basic minimum wage be altered. Unimportant modifications would be avoided by providing that no variation in the minimum wage should take place unless production showed an increase or decrease of a given percentage, say 3 per cent.

Objections have been raised to the system of adjustment on the basis of statistics of past production. It may be unsatisfactory to raise wages at the beginning of 1927 merely because production during 1926 was higher than in previous years. Should there be a decline in productivity during 1927, industry would experience difficulty in paying the higher wages. In order to avoid this difficulty the proposal has been made that statistics of past productivity should be combined with an index of prospective productivity, which would give an indication as to probable conditions during the period in which the wages will be paid.

There has been an important development in recent years of indices of prospective productivity, in other words, of economic barometers.[1] The progress made is not yet sufficient to warrant their use as a regular determining factor, although the indications they give might be taken into consideration when wages are being adjusted. Also economic barometers might be used to modify the rigid application of a cost of living sliding scale. The statistics of the cost of living might show a fall of 10 per cent. during the past period. If, however, the economic barometer should point to a rise in prices during the next period, it might be advisable not to effect the reduction in wages according to the cost of living sliding scale. To this extent account would be taken of the business cycle.

Proposals on the lines under consideration have been made in the United States and in Australia. In the United States the adoption of the principle that wages

[1] The best-known economic barometers are those published by the Harvard University Committee on Economic Research and the London and Cambridge Economic Service. Various other economic barometers are also constructed in the United States. The Federation of British Industries publishes a barometer ; while in France and Belgium barometers are constructed. It is probable that in a number of other countries the compilation and scientific combination of statistical series with the object of enabling tentative forecasts to be made of industrial conditions will before long be undertaken. For a short account of the objects and methods of compilation of economic barometers see : International Labour Office : Studies and Reports, Series N (Statistics), No. 5, *Economic Barometers :* a Report submitted to the Economic Committee of the League of Nations, Geneva, 1924.

should be adjusted to changes in the product of the whole of industry has been advocated to some extent by the Trade Unions. A detailed memorandum on the subject was submitted to the House of Representatives Committee on Labor by an association of machinists in connection with a Bill to create a wage board for employees in naval dockyards and arsenals.[1] The essential feature of the proposal was the construction of an index of *per capita* production and the adjustment of wages to the changes indicated.

More elaborate is the proposal of the Economic Commission on the Queensland Basic Wage appointed at the end of 1924 by the Queensland Court of Industrial Arbitration.[2] In its Report the Commission recommended that " the chief guide to be followed by the Court in declaring a Standard Basic Wage for industries of ' average prosperity ' should be the capacity of the industry to pay," and that at different dates changes in " capacity to pay should be determined from figures showing changes in income per head, past production per head, and future production per head." In other words, an index of capacity to pay would be constructed by combining three separate series of statistics : first, an index of *per capita* income calculated from income tax statistics, together with data for persons who do not pay income tax, i.e.

[1] Report presented to the House Committee on Labor, 67th Congress, 2nd Session (1922). See H. Feis, *Principles of Wage Settlement*, p. 402.

[2] *The Queensland Industrial Gazette*, vol. X, No. 3, March 24th, 1925, pp. 185–214.

mainly wage-earners ; [1] second, an index of *per capita* material production based on statistics of the total value of material production in the chief industries and the number of persons employed ; third, an index of prospective production during the months immediately ahead, constructed from data of the volume and value of stocks of raw materials together with the prices of the stocks and shares of the Government and of business companies as shown by Stock Exchange quotations.

Broadly speaking, the general level of wages in any country does vary in accordance with changes in the national dividend. The studies of Professor Bowley and Dr. King mentioned in the preceding chapter indicate this tendency for Great Britain and the United States. Less complete information available for Australia, Holland, and other countries points in the same direction. The value of the proposal under consideration is, however, that minimum wages, instead of being varied by the rough interplay of forces and the relative strengths and tactical advantages of rival organisations, with all the friction and loss involved in the struggle, would be adjusted by means of a scientific measure of changes in the nation's income.

As the efficiency of industry improves it is essential

---

[1] For practical reasons the Commission found that, at present, owing to the absence in Queensland of the information necessary for the construction of an index of income per head, the index of capacity to pay could be constructed from the indices of past and prospective production only.

that real wages should increase. The volume of production depends primarily on ability to market the product. As the demand of the wage-earners is one of the chief constituents of total demand, it would be almost impossible to market an increased volume of goods per head without an increase in real wages. It is immaterial from this point of view whether the rise in real wages results from an increase in money wages or from a fall in prices.

The strict application of the principle of adjusting real wages to changes in the total productivity of industry implies that the share of the product of industry received by the workers remains unchanged. Whatever may be said in favour of changes in the proportion of the national dividend which goes to the workers, it is desirable that any general increase in productivity should be accompanied by a corresponding rise in real wages.

To summarise the conclusions of the preceding sections, in each country there should be fixed a limit below which no wage should fall. This minimum should be based on the capacity to pay of industry in general. In practice, the most satisfactory method of determining the minimum would be to fix it at a given proportion, e.g. 80 per cent., of the average wage paid to unskilled workers in a number of the chief industries of the country. Since the minimum wage is to be based on the capacity to pay of industry in general, changes in the productivity of industry should be accompanied by corresponding changes in the minimum wage. These adjustments would be made by means of an index of *per capita* material production.

PRELIMINARY MEASURES.

The programme outlined above, involving as it does the fixing of a national minimum real wage, must not be regarded as immediately attainable but as the aim of legislation and administrative measures.[1] Instead of at once declaring a national minimum in any country, the first step is the establishment of machinery with the object of improving the wages of workers in a few of the lowest paid unorganised industries. This improvement could be effected by boards set up separately in each industry, no attempt being made to fix uniform wage rates in the different industries. The number of boards could be gradually increased until the system applied to all unorganised industries in which the wages of unskilled workers were considerably below the general level. An alternative method is the fixing of minimum rates in different industries by a Central Commission on the advice of a representative board in each industry.[2]

If boards are set up in different industries many of the problems with which they deal are similar. The board in one industry is influenced by the methods

[1] In certain countries with widely differing economic regions several real minima may be necessary.
[2] The main features of different types of wage-fixing machinery are outlined in Chapter X.

adopted by other boards, and in fixing minimum rates reference is made to rates in other industries, especially those in which boards have been established. In this way a tendency for inequalities to be diminished operates, which could be strengthened by systematic co-ordination between the various boards. Maximum co-ordination is possible if rates in different industries are fixed by a Central Commission.

In Great Britain a measure of co-ordination of the work of different Trade Boards is effected by the Ministry of Labour, and by a number of employers' and workers' representatives as well as of disinterested ("appointed") members sitting on several boards. Also when a board is considering what minimum wages to fix, reference is frequently made to the minimum rates fixed by other boards. Consequently not only have the boards been instrumental in raising the wages of workers in the industries covered, but there has been a tendency for the disparity from one industry to another to be decreased. An examination of the general minimum time rates fixed by British Trade Boards for the lowest grades of experienced male and female workers shows comparatively small differences from one industry to another. About 80 per cent. of the rates in force for male workers at the beginning of 1926 were from 11d. to 1s. 2d. per hour, or from 44s. to 56s. for a week of 48 hours. In the case of female workers nearly 90 per cent. of the rates were from 6¼d. to 7½d. per hour, or 25s. to 30s. for a week of 48 hours. Six rates for male workers were below 11d. per hour, the lowest being 10d ; only one rate for female workers was below 6¼d. per hour.[1] With a strengthening of co-ordinating tendencies it should be possible in the course of a few years to reduce the differences between the wages of unskilled workers in the industries covered by Trade Boards till an effective national minimum could be declared without imposing undue strain on any industry. A Central Commission would be necessary for the declaration of this minimum.

The object of Trade Boards or a Central Commission in any country should be not merely to raise the wages of unskilled workers in the different industries but, by narrowing the range of those wages, to prepare the way for the adoption of a national minimum. In industries in which wages are below the level determined according to the method suggested in Section I of this chapter, the task of minimum wage machinery should be to raise wages to that amount. If after a reasonable time this objective has not been attained such a wage should nevertheless be then declared as a national minimum applicable to all industries.[2]

National minimum wages already exist in New Zealand and in various States in Australia ; wages of State-wide application have been fixed for women in

[1] *Eighteenth Abstract of Labour Statistics of the United Kingdom* (Cd. 2740, London, 1926), p. 109.

[2] The conditions of agricultural workers differ to such an extent from those of industrial workers that special measures for the fixing of minimum wages for workers in agriculture will often be necessary.

certain States of the United States of America.   In
Great Britain in 1919 a Committee of the National
Industrial Conference affirmed the principle of national
minimum rates of wages, and a Government Bill was
subsequently introduced for the appointment of a
Commission to enquire into and decide what such
minimum rates should be, "regard being had to the
cost of living in the various districts."   No progress
was made with this Bill, and similar measures introduced in Parliament more recently have met with no
success.   The principle of the national minimum is,
however, more widely supported in Great Britain than
might at first be thought.   Thus, for example, in a
leading article on "The Basis of Wages" published in
The Times, June 16th, 1925, the opinion was expressed
that "there is a general agreement that a wage of
somewhere about the lowest figure enforced by Trade
Boards should be a first charge on any industry." [1]

The fixing of a national minimum would not do
away with the need for Trade Boards or other
machinery for fixing minimum rates in various industries.   It would still be necessary for wages to be
regulated in industries in which employers and workers
were not well organised, and in which wages were

[1] According to information published in the *Eighteenth
Abstract of Labour Statistics of the United Kingdom*, the
lowest figure fixed by any Trade Board at the beginning of
1926 was 10d. per hour, or 40s. per week of 48 hours, for
unskilled adult male workers, and 6¼d. per hour, or 25s. per
week of 48 hours, for unskilled adult female workers (apart
from an exceptionally low rate of 5½d. per hour fixed by one
board for adult women in the Orkney and Shetland Islands
only).

consequently low. The machinery set up would as far as possible fix rates of wages of unskilled workers above the national minimum, and determine the rates of wages of various grades of skilled workers. It would also deal with piece rates, special rates for learners, etc. Its function would be to determine wages and other conditions of labour in unorganised trades, thus providing a substitute for collective agreements reached in the organised industries.

Exceptions to the general minimum time rate may be necessary in two cases. First, a somewhat lower minimum may be allowed to help an industry during an experimental period or to tide over other temporary periods of difficulty. Special measures may be necessary in the case of an industry suffering from severe foreign competition. The fixing of lower wages to meet such circumstances should be agreed to only as a temporary measure, and the period during which this exceptional treatment would operate should be fixed as definitely as possible. The decision to fix wages below the general minimum should be made only after a full examination of the financial condition and prospects of the industry.

The second class of exceptions to the general minimum time rate is that of sub-normal workers who by reason of some defect are below the ordinary level, of efficiency. The question of allowing such workers to be employed at wages below the general minimum is considered in some detail in a later chapter.

CHAPTER VII

PROVISION FOR THE WORKER'S FAMILY

IN previous chapters reference has been made to the workers' demand for a living wage, but although mention has been made of laws which provide for the fixing for adult male workers of minimum wages adequate for a man with wife and three children, there has been no attempt to examine whether or not such a basis be reasonable. In the present chapter this attempt is made.

The worker regards his wage not merely as payment for work done but also as the means of supplying his needs and those of his dependants. These requirements are variable. Many unmarried workers have only themselves to maintain. Other workers have large families to support. Clearly a wage which is more than sufficient to supply the needs of the former may be inadequate for the latter.

Under the systems of wage payment applied in most countries no account is taken of the differing needs of the workers. Generally workers engaged on similar work in a given establishment or district receive the same rate of wage, without regard to the fact that some are unmarried, while others have families to support. In some occupations a time basis is adopted, the workers being paid so much per hour, per day, or per week. In other occupations, output forms the basis, so much per piece being paid. Neither system takes account of differences in needs ; the principle of " equal pay for equal work " is applied.

In wage negotiations for the fixing of time or piece rates the workers often claim that the rates must be sufficient to supply family needs. Generally they demand a wage adequate for a family of average size ; almost always such a family is regarded as consisting of husband, wife, and three dependent children. Since, however, the wage applies equally to all workers of given grade irrespective of the numbers of their dependants, the fixing of the wage on the basis of the requirements of an average family involves no breach of the principle of " equal pay for equal work."

If a family of husband, wife, and three dependent children be typical, and the number of families with more or fewer children be small, then the system of fixing wages on the basis of a five-member family will give fairly satisfactory results. Statistics show, however, that the family of five is not typical. In England and Wales, according to the 1921 Census, 26·6 per cent. of all adult males twenty years of age and over were unmarried. The following figures show the percentages for married men without children and with children under sixteen years of age :—

	Per cent.
Without children, or did not furnish information ..	43
With one child	23
With two children	15
With three children	9
With four or more children	10

The average number of children under sixteen years of age per married worker was only 1·27, and the average per man about one child.[1]

In such conditions the payment to all workers of a wage adequate for a family of five implies that large numbers of workers enjoy a surplus over subsistence requirements. For a comparatively small percentage of workers the wage is just adequate, while for families with more than three children there is insufficient provision. A similar criticism can be directed against any system whereby workers are paid at a flat rate. Only by variation according to needs can the difficulty be removed.

The case against the system of payment at a flat rate to all workers of given grade is not strong where the standard of living provided by the wages is high. If the wage provides a good standard of comfort for a family of five, then larger families, although unable to enjoy equal comforts, will not be deprived of necessaries. Where the standard of living provided by the

[1] Professor Paul H. Douglas, in an article " Is the Family of Five Typical ? " gives figures for France, Belgium, India, and the United States, as well as for Great Britain, which show that in none of these countries does the number of families with three dependent children exceed 20 per cent. of the total number of families covered by the statistics. The great majority of families, in some countries more than 80 per cent., have fewer than three dependent children (*Quarterly Publication of the American Statistical Association,* September 1924, pp. 314–28).

Mr. A. B. Piddington, K.C., in *The Next Step : a Basic Family Income,* Melbourne, 1922, shows that in Australia the family of five is not typical.

wage is low, the case against the system of equal pay is strongest. In low-paid industries the wage may be adequate only for a worker with wife and one child ; workers without children enjoy a surplus over mere subsistence requirements, while those with large families suffer privation. To avoid the defects of the system of equal pay, that of "payment according to need," often known as the "family allowance system," has been adopted in some countries and advocated in others.

It is necessary to examine this system at some length, as its adoption would fundamentally affect the whole range of wage regulation.

THE FAMILY ALLOWANCE SYSTEM.[1]

This system implies an improvement in the distribution of that part of the national dividend which is paid to the workers. It is this improvement which provides family allowance advocates with their strongest argument. The introduction of the system need involve no change in the total wage bill, but be merely a redistribution by which the resources of workers whose families are larger than the average are increased at the expense of workers with families

[1] Details of the application of the family allowance system in various countries are given in International Labour Office Studies and Reports, Series D, No. 13, *Family Allowances,* Geneva, 1924. The case in favour of the system is developed by Miss Eleanor F. Rathbone in her book, *The Disinherited Family,* London, 1924, and by Professor Paul H. Douglas in *Wages and the Family,* Chicago, 1925.

smaller than the average. As indicated later, however, the family allowance system has sometimes been adopted to meet a reduction in total real wages. In such circumstances the change in the method of distribution serves to mitigate the effects of the fall in real wages by concentrating the reduction on those with few dependants. As was stated by the Coal Commission in its Report, " The introduction of a system of children's allowances will raise the standard of living if the total wage bill remains unchanged, and may neutralise largely or completely any evil effects that would otherwise result from a fall of wages." [1]

The essential features of a complete system of payment according to need are the payment of an equal wage to all workers of given grade, together with allowances for the maintenance of the wife and children of the married worker. The greater the number of dependants, the higher the total amount of the allowances. If the allowances be adequate for the maintenance of dependants, the worker will have himself alone to provide for out of his wage.

In practice nowhere does a complete system of family allowances appear to have been applied. The allowances have usually been inadequate for the maintenance of the dependants in respect of whom they have been paid. Also, in many cases, allowances have been paid for children but not for the wife.

---

[1] *Report of the Royal Commission on the Coal Industry* (*1925*), Cd. 2600, London, 1926, vol. 1, p. 162 ; see also p. 235.

Sometimes they have been paid only for families over a given size, e.g. with more than two children.

The principle of payment according to need was partially applied in most European countries during the war and in the years immediately following its termination.[1] In many cases the system developed from the practice of meeting the rise in prices by adding to basic wages cost of living bonuses differentiated according to family needs. This practice served to mitigate the worst effects of the fall in real wages which accompanied the depreciation of the currency. However, it was regarded in a number of countries as a means of dealing with exceptional conditions, and not as a permanent method of providing for workers' dependants. Therefore, when more normal conditions were restored, the family allowance system declined in importance in many countries. Especially in Scandinavian countries, Switzerland, and Italy there was a rapid return to the system of equal pay for equal work. From 1921 onwards the family allowance system ceased to be applied in these countries for workers in private industry, although in some of them it was retained in the public administrative services. In Czechoslovakia also the system declined rapidly in importance during 1921 and 1922, although it continues to be applied in certain industries. In Austria and Poland, currency depreciation and the

---

[1] Even before the war the principle had been adopted in a few cases. Thus in France allowances for dependants were paid to State employees in some of the public administrative services.

consequent rise in prices continued for a period after comparative stability had been reached in the countries already mentioned, but, after more stable conditions were restored, the system of family allowances received less and less application. Finally, in Germany, where the principle of payment according to need had received extensive application during the period of inflation, a marked reversion to the system of equal pay followed the stabilisation of the currency at the end of 1923.[1]

In the countries mentioned in the preceding paragraph the family allowance system has been mainly a temporary expedient, although, once introduced, probably it will not altogether disappear. Very different is the situation in France, where, although the system was introduced during the war for similar reasons to those which led to its adoption elsewhere, there are special conditions which indicate greater possibilities of permanence. The system has been welcomed as a means of increasing the birth-rate, and its development is encouraged with the object of maintaining or increasing the population. From 1920 onwards the system has steadily increased in importance, both as regards numbers of workers covered and rates of allowances paid.[2] In Belgium, largely in

[1] An article by Dr. Busze comparing the extent of application of the family allowance system in Germany in 1922–3 and two years later was published in the *Reichsarbeitsblatt*, January 24th, 1926.

[2] In May 1926, according to a Report presented to the Sixth National Congress of Equalisation Funds by M. Bonvoisin,

imitation of France, an important development began in the autumn of 1922, and continued throughout 1923. Subsequent extension was less rapid, but the system established shows signs of permanence.[1] In other countries of continental Europe the payment of family allowances has developed to some extent, e.g. in Holland, the Serb-Croat-Slovene Kingdom, and Rumania.

Propaganda in favour of the family allowance system has been undertaken in Great Britain, Australia, and, less extensively, in the United States. In these countries the case for the payment of family allowances is not based on the necessity of dealing with an exceptional situation nor on a desire to increase the birth-rate. It is based mainly on the argument that in any community a higher general standard of living can be attained under the family allowance system than under that of "equal pay."

METHODS OF PROVIDING FAMILY ALLOWANCES.

Family allowances may be provided out of funds supplied by the workers, the employers, or the State,

Director of the Comité Central des Allocations Familiales, the number of workers in establishments in private industry which paid family allowances was 2,600,000. To these should be added about a million manual and non-manual workers covered by the family allowance system in public administrative services (*La Journée Industrielle*, May 16th–17th, 1926).

[1] At the end of 1925 the number of workers in private industry covered by the system was over 300,000, or more than 20 per cent. of all such workers. In addition, family allowances were paid in public administrative services. (*Bulletin du Comité Central Industriel de Belgique*, November 11th, 1925, pp. 886–92.)

or by any combination of these three. A group of workers, e.g. members of a Trade Union, might agree that each worker should contribute regularly a given sum to a fund from which the allowances would be paid.[1] In practice family allowances are generally paid out of sums provided by the employers. Almost always provision by employers has been voluntary, either in accordance with collective agreements or solely on the initiative of the employers. In Central European and Scandinavian countries applications of the family allowance system have generally been based on collective agreements. In France and Belgium the employers have almost always introduced the system on their own initiative with little or no regard to the views of the workers' organisations.

Where employers pay family allowances directly to their workpeople, whether in accordance with the terms of collective agreements or on their own initiative, there is the danger that they may dismiss workers with families, especially those with large families, and replace them, as far as possible, by unmarried workers. By this means the amount paid in allowances will be reduced. The most satisfactory way of removing this danger is to adopt the equalisation fund system. Instead of allowances being paid directly to the worker,

[1] In Belgium the Confederation of Christian Trade Unions decided, in 1924, to establish a fund from which children's allowances would be paid to members of affiliated unions. The fund was to be maintained by payments by affiliated unions of a sum of 275 francs per member per annum. Allowances were to be paid in respect of children under sixteen years of age, from the third child (*Revue de Travail*, March 31st, 1924).

the employers of a given industry or district constitute a common fund from which allowances are paid. The contributions of each employer to the fund are based on some factor not proportionate to the number of his workers' children. Among such factors are the total number of his workers and his total wage bill. Equalisation funds on these lines have developed to an important extent in France and Belgium, and appear to have been successful in preventing discrimination against workers with large families.[1] In Germany, family allowances have generally been paid directly, few equalisation funds having been set up. Nevertheless, there has been little discrimination against married workers, partly, no doubt, because the allowances have usually been small in amount and therefore the inducement to prefer unmarried workers slight.

Legislation has been proposed in various countries with the object of making compulsory the payment of family allowances out of equalisation funds maintained by contributions from employers. Especially in France, the Commonwealth of Australia, and the State of New South Wales such measures have been discussed. In France a law was passed in December 1922 making the payment of allowances and membership of an equalisation fund obligatory on employers engaged on State contracts. In Austria a law passed at the end

[1] In France, in May 1926, the number of equalisation funds was 195, covering 14,000 establishments with 1,300,000 workers. In Belgium, at the beginning of 1926, the number of funds associated with the Comité d'Etudes des Allocations Familiales was 12, covering 773 establishments with over 150,000 workers.

of 1921 introduced a general system of family allowances paid by employers through the intermediary of
district equalisation funds.[1] By the autumn of 1922,
owing to currency depreciation, the real value of the
allowances became negligible, as they were not adjusted to the change in the value of the monetary
unit.   In March 1926 the system came to an end with
the expiration of the law.

In certain European countries and in Australia
many workers' organisations advocate the provision
of family allowances out of State revenues.   In
France a law of July 22nd, 1923, provides for the
payment of allowances by the State in respect of all
children after the third under thirteen years of age.
In this case the connection with the wage problem is
remote, the main object of the law being to encourage
an increase in the birth-rate.   In New Zealand in
1926, an Act was passed to provide family allowances
out of State revenues.   (See page 119.) One other
method of providing sums necessary for the payment
of family allowances may be mentioned, that of divid-
ing the cost between the State, the employers, and the
workers.   Such a system could be organised on similar
lines to those adopted for unemployment and other
forms of social insurance.[2]

---

[1] The system was introduced to facilitate the abolition
of food subsidies which had previously been paid. It was
generally regarded as a temporary expedient.

[2] This method has been advocated by Mr. J. L. Cohen in
*Family Income Insurance : a Scheme of Family Endowment
by the Method of Insurance*, London, 1926.

EFFECT ON POPULATION.

Although the system of family allowances provides a better distribution of resources than that of equal pay, this does not prove the desirability of introducing the system. Enquiry must be made into the reactions which are likely to follow its adoption. Chief among these is the effect on population.

In any country already sufficiently populated a system leading to an increase in the birth-rate would tend to result in a reduction in the average standard of living. In the case of Great Britain the view is widely held that, with existing methods of production, any considerable increase in population would be undesirable. Therefore the introduction of the family allowance system would be unsatisfactory if it would lead to an increase in population. Although its adoption would result in improved distribution, this advantage would be outweighed in the course of time by the lowering of the standard of living which would result from the pressure of an increased population on the resources available.

In France, where an increase in the birth-rate is much desired, the family allowance system is regarded as an important means to this end. In Great Britain advocates of family allowances claim that the system would substantially lower the birth-rate of the poorer wage-earning classes, that it would probably slightly raise the birth-rate of the artisan and lower middle classes, and that it would have practically no effect on

the birth-rate of the wealthy classes.[1] This conclusion is based mainly on the fact that the birth-rate
is often less among classes whose standard of living is
high than among classes with a low standard. Advocates of the system believe that at present, in the case
of the classes with the lowest incomes, "the hopeless-
ness of a proper discharge of parental obligations
breeds a recklessness in incurring them." They consider that the proper discharge of parental obligations would be facilitated by a system of family
allowances, and this might result in a reduction in the
birth-rate among the lowest paid groups. In the case
of the artisan and lower middle classes foresight is
generally exercised, and the parents endeavour to
restrict their families to a size appropriate to their
income. It is thought that some increase in the birth-
rate of these classes would follow the removal of the
"economic restriction on parenthood" resulting from
the introduction of a system of family allowances.

Thus there are two views as to the effect of a system
of family allowances on population. Which is cor-
rect ? To this question no satisfactory answer is forth-
coming. The problem is examined in a report prepared
by the International Labour Office early in 1926 on
"The Effects of Family Allowances and the Relation
between the Provision of Family Allowances and
Social Insurance." The investigations on which the
report is based were limited to France and Belgium,
"the only countries for which there appeared any

[1] *The Disinherited Family*, by Eleanor F. Rathbone, p. 247.

possibility of securing a basis for even tentative conclusions as to the effect of family allowances." In the case of Belgium, enquiry showed that the system is too recent a development to permit of definite conclusions regarding its effect on the birth-rate. For France the report states that the information available is very inconclusive, and reference is made to the difficulty of distinguishing the influence on the birth-rate of the payment of family allowances from that of other factors.[1]

The effect of family allowances on the birth-rate will depend to a considerable extent on the amounts paid and the system of payment. Large allowances paid on an ascending scale, i.e. with a higher amount for each succeeding child, would probably cause an increase in the birth-rate. In the different countries which have introduced the system of family allowances the amounts paid have generally been far from covering the whole cost of maintenance of children. In France, in May 1926, the average rates of allowance based on the scales of the thirty chief equalisation funds, whose payments represent 80 per cent. of total allowances, were as tabulated below.[2] Figures are also

---

[1] The report was based mainly on information compiled by the French Comité Central des Allocations Familiales.

[2] Figures from the Report to the Sixth National Congress of Equalisation Funds by M. Bonvoisin, Director of the Comité Central des Allocations Familiales (*La Journée Industrielle*, May 16th–17th, 1926). Certain equalisation funds pay allowances at rates considerably above the average. The Michelin Company pays allowances according to a high scale, i.e. 75 francs for the first child, 75 francs for the second, 150 francs

given of the percentage additions which the allowances make to the wages of an adult workman with a wage of 750 francs per month.

	Average Allowance per Month.	Percentage Addition to Wage of 750 Francs per Month.
	Francs.	
For 1 child	25·23	3½
For 2 children	63·02	8½
For 3 children	109·47	14½
For 4 children	173·16	23
For 5 children	240·34	32
For 6 children	318·00	42

Although important, the amounts paid in allowances are considerably below the cost of maintenance. It may be estimated that in France, at the beginning of 1926, the average costs of maintaining children of various ages were [1] :—

Children under one year of age—about 125 francs per month ;

Children one to three years of age—about 125–250 francs per month ;

Children over three years of age—250–365 francs per month.

for the third, and 100 francs for the fourth and succeeding children. Statistics have been compiled which seem to show that the payment of these allowances has resulted in an increase in the birth-rate among workers in Michelin undertakings.

[1] These estimates are based on figures for 1923 and 1924 given in a report on the cost of the birth and maintenance of children by M. Dupont, Director of the Lille Textile Family Allowance Fund (Official Record of the Fourth National Congress of Equalisation Funds). Adjustment has been made to allow for the changes in the cost of living.

In Belgium the scales of allowances are generally lower than those of France. In Germany only in a few occupations and industries, including State employment and coal-mining in certain districts, do the allowances constitute an important addition to the wage. In no country have allowances adequate for maintenance been paid.

CONCLUSIONS.

The family allowance system has been examined in some detail on account of its close relation to various wage problems and because it is intimately connected with one of the main purposes for which minimum wages are fixed. The minimum wage principle is applied because the standard of living of certain groups of workers is low. The low standard is due in some cases to the low productivity of the industry. In other words, the amount available for distribution as wages is inadequate. By the improved distribution which the family allowance system implies the amount available might become adequate for a reasonable standard of living.

Against this advantage there are important defects. However, for one group of workers the balance is on the side of the family allowance system. This group consists of workers whose wages are below the level considered reasonable in relation to the general standard of living of the community. For such workers the institution of a system of family allowances

is desirable. The greatest poverty is experienced by
workers in this group who have large families. The
productivity of the industries concerned is at present
inadequate satisfactorily to supply their needs if the
system of equal pay is retained. By introducing the
family allowance system the same total wages bill
would provide a more satisfactory standard of living,
and poverty would be diminished.

Objection is raised to the application of the system
to the lowest paid workers on the ground that it would
lead to an increase in the birth-rate of the least desirable class of the community. But the birth-rate of
this class is already high. Poverty has not caused the
restraint that might have been expected, and it is
unlikely that a system of allowances on a descending
scale would lead to any considerable increase in the
birth-rate.

A further objection is raised that provision of
allowances for the children of the lowest paid classes of
workers would encourage laziness. This might be the
case if the allowances were not related to employment ;
for example, if they were paid by the State. On the
other hand, if payment of allowances and wage ceased
when the worker was out of a job, there would be every
inducement to remain in employment.

The adoption of the family allowance system for the
class under consideration would be merely an extension
of a system already applied for the prevention of
poverty, e.g. in the case of poor relief and unemployment benefits. In outdoor relief the principle of

payment according to need is adopted. Also in a number of countries unemployment insurance benefits are varied according to size of family. In Germany and certain other countries, as has been seen, the family allowance system was applied during and since the war to mitigate the effects of the low level of real wages consequent upon currency depreciation. An Act passed by the New Zealand Legislature in 1926 provides for the payment of allowances to those with large families and small incomes; allowances of 2s. per week are to be paid in respect of each child under fifteen years of age in families with more than two children, provided the average income of the family, exclusive of the allowances, does not exceed £4 per week.[1] In each of these cases the object in view in adopting the system of payment according to needs has been to prevent misery. One of the objects of the British Coal Commission in proposing the adoption of the family allowance system for coal-miners was to diminish the harmful effects of the reduction in wages which the economic conditions of the industry appeared to demand.

The adoption of the family allowance system is advocated above as a means of preventing privation and distress among workers with unduly low wages. In the case of other groups than the lowest paid, most workers have a margin above mere subsistence. Workers with large families are obliged to sacrifice

---

[1] To very large families allowances may be paid though income exceeds £4 per week.

comforts during the years when their children are dependent. On the other hand, they enjoy a higher standard of living before marriage and when their children become self-supporting. The family allowance system would increase the standard of living of the worker during the period of dependence of his children at the expense of a lower standard before and after that period, and also at the expense of the worker with few or no children.

The effects of family allowances on population become of outstanding importance when it is proposed to apply the system to a large section of the community. In view of the uncertainty regarding these effects the family allowance system, if it is to be applied on a scale considerably wider than to a comparatively small group of workers whose wages are unduly low, should be introduced experimentally on a voluntary basis by agreement between employers and workers, and not by a State-established system. The introduction by a State already sufficiently populated of a scheme for the payment of allowances *adequate* for the maintenance of *all* children, or of the children of large classes of the community, would be inadvisable. By whatever system such a scheme would be financed, estimates would be essential of the annual amounts required to provide the allowances for a period of years. In making these estimates it would be necessary to know the probable number of children in respect of whom allowances would be paid, and the average amount of the allowance. The latter of these elements would be known, but it would be impossible to make a reasonably accurate forecast of the number of children there would be in a community after a period of years during which allowances adequate for maintenance had been paid. The number would depend on the effects of the system on the birth-rate and on the child mortality rate. At present any estimate on these lines would be largely guess-work.

To sum up, the family allowance system is desirable as a means of preventing privation among a comparatively small group of workers whose wages are exceptionally low. Its value in the case of other groups of workers depends to a large extent on its effects on population, regarding which there is at present little satisfactory evidence.

CHAPTER VIII

RELATION BETWEEN THE WAGES OF MEN AND WOMEN

In previous chapters the general problems of minimum wages have been examined, and also the special problem of provision for the worker's dependants. Reference has been made mainly to the wages of adult male workers. However, many minimum wage authorities are required to fix rates for both sexes. It is therefore necessary to consider the principles which should be adopted in determining the relation between the wages of men and women. To make a detailed survey of the whole subject would be outside the scope of the present volume.[1] All that is here attempted is to indicate some of its chief features.

There are two more or less separate problems : that of men and women engaged side by side on identical work, and that where the two sexes work in different occupations. The number of occupations where men and women are employed on work of exactly the same kind is small. Usually, even where men and women are engaged together in the same workshop, the men

---

[1] The problem is treated in detail in the *Report of the War Cabinet Committee on Women in Industry*, London, 1919 (Cd. 135). Mention may also be made of *Die Ursachen der ungleichen Entlohnung von Männer- und Frauenarbeit*, by Alice Salomon, Leipzig, 1906, and *L'égalité des salaires ; à travail égal salaire égal ?* by Françoise Delavant, Paris, 1916.

become specialised on one type of work and the women on another in consequence of differences in aptitude. The claim that the principle of equal pay for equal work should be applied can be reasonably made only if the work is similar. Where the type of work differs the claim would be meaningless, there being no basis for determining equality of work. Therefore, where the work is dissimilar, and this is the case in the great majority of trades, some other principle must be adopted. For basic rates the relation is determined in some countries by the living wage principle, interpreted according to the general productivity of industry as a whole. In such countries rates above the basic minima, and in other countries both basic and higher rates, are fixed mainly according to the capacity of each separate industry. The relation between the wages of men and women in these cases is therefore determined according to the law of demand and supply. This results in relations which vary from one industry to another. The notes which follow deal with the principle which leads to a more definite relationship, namely, " The living wage basis." The principle of " Equal pay for equal work " is also examined.

THE LIVING WAGE BASIS.

The cost of maintenance for a woman differs little from that for a man. Her food requirements are lower on the average ; the results of medical research show the needs of a woman to be about 80 to 90 per cent.

of those of a man.[1] For clothing, housing accommodation, fuel, light, and other groups of expenditure the requirements of a woman are approximately equal to, or, for certain of these groups, somewhat higher than those of a man. It follows that, from the point of view of their own requirements, there is a strong presumption in favour of an appropriate equality in the wages of the two sexes. Figures below, based on an official enquiry, show the total cost of the budget necessary to maintain in health and decency a single man and a single woman in the United States Government clerical service at the level of prices in August and September 1919. The amount necessary, with very economical management, for the maintenance in health and decency of a family of the low-salaried Government clerk class consisting of husband, wife, and three children under fourteen years of age is also given.[2] The figures do not include provision for saving.

	Annual Cost of Maintenance in Dollars.	Relative Figures.
Single man　..　　..　　..	961·41	100
Single woman ..　　..　　..	1,037·20	108
Family of five ..　　..　　..	2,015·56	210

[1] Such percentages are shown by Engel's "quet" scale, by Atwater's scale, and by the scales used in connection with family budget enquiries in Germany, the United States, and Australia. These scales are based entirely or mainly on food.

[2] *United States Monthly Labor Review*, December 1919, p. 28, and January 1920, p. 35. The amount necessary, with ordinary management, for a family of five was $2,262·47 per annum.

The conventional requirements of women in Government clerical service are no doubt partly responsible for the figure for a woman being higher than that for a man. At the present standards of manual workers in Western countries, the relation between the requirements of men and women would probably be one of equality. At the level for mere subsistence and physical efficiency, the requirements of a man would be slightly higher than those of a woman.

Although there is an approximate equality between the cost of maintenance of a man and of a woman, the wages of men when determined in accordance with the living wage principle are generally fixed at rates considerably higher than those of women. The reason given is that a large proportion of adult male workers are responsible for the maintenance of a wife and children, whereas the proportion of women who have dependants is comparatively small. The man's living wage is fixed for the maintenance of a family of average size, while the woman's living wage is based on the requirements of a woman maintaining herself, but without dependants. This relation is generally adopted in basic wage declarations in Australia. In Canada and the United States, where minimum wage fixing bodies are in most cases required to fix the wages of women workers only, the basis adopted is the sum required by a woman living away from home, but without dependants.

This method of determining the relation between the living wages of men and women is not free from objection.   As was seen in the previous chapter, a considerable proportion of adult male workers have no family obligations.   On the other hand, a proportion of women have dependants.   The difficulties due to the maintenance of dependants would be largely removed by the adoption of the family allowance system.   Also, as pointed out by family allowance advocates, this system would facilitate the adoption of the principle of equal pay for equal work between men and women by removing the necessity that the man's wage should be adequate for the maintenance of a family.

Where the family allowance system is not introduced, and there are indications in many countries that for a long period its adoption in industry is not likely to become general, the most satisfactory alternative is that indicated above, namely, for a man a basic wage adequate for a family of average size, and for a woman a basic wage sufficient for her own maintenance without dependants.   Apart from the family allowance system, this method is the nearest rough approximation to reality.

In the previous chapter figures from the British Census of 1921 were quoted, showing that in England and Wales 73·4 per cent. of adult males twenty years of age and over were married.   Indications were also given as to the number of children.   The extent to which families in certain countries are maintained by the earnings of the husband is indicated by the table opposite, which gives the results of official enquiries into the budgets mainly of working-class families.

PROPORTIONS OF TOTAL FAMILY INCOME DERIVED FROM VARIOUS SOURCES.

Country.	Date of Enquiry.	Number of Families.	Proportion of Total Income formed by—			
			Earnings of Husband.	Earnings of Wife.	Earnings of Children.	Other Income.[1]
			Per cent.	Per cent.	Per cent.	Per cent.
Austria	1912–14	117	79·5	8·4	6·1	6·0
Esthonia (Tallin) ..	1925	176	77·5	6·2	6·9	9·4
Germany	1907	852	84·7	2·7	1·7	10·9
India (Bombay) ..	1921–22	2,473	80·6	13·3	2·3	3·8
Norway	1918–19	82	86·4	2·5	7·2	3·9
Russia (Moscow) ..	Nov. 1925	—	73·9	17·1 [2]	—	9·0
Sweden	1913–14	1,355	87·3	2·2	3·0	7·5
Switzerland [3] ..	1921	122	80·5	4·0	4·5	11·0
United States ..	1918–19	12,096	89·2	0·9	5·9	4·0

[1] Including income from boarders and lodgers.　　[2] Including earnings of children.
[3] Families of skilled workers.

The statistics show that on the average, in most of the countries covered, families are maintained to the extent of about 80 to 90 per cent. by the earnings of the husband. Unfortunately, similar figures are not available for Great Britain, where, hitherto, in family budget enquiries statistics of income classified according to source have not been obtained.[1]

In the case of women workers the number with dependants is comparatively small, while among women workers with dependants the great majority maintain only one person, partially or wholly. Mr. B. S. Rowntree, in *The Human Needs of Labour*, gives figures for England which show that, among women workers eighteen years of age and over covered by the investigation, five out of six had no dependants at all. Other investigations have been conducted with varying results.[2] They generally seem to show that the number of women workers in English towns responsible for the maintenance, partially or wholly, of dependants does not exceed about one in

---

[1] Mr. B. S. Rowntree in *Poverty : a Study of Town Life* gives figures obtained in an investigation conducted in York in 1899 which show that, at that date, male heads of households contributed, on an average, 74·3 per cent. of the total sum earned per family.

[2] Reference may be made to statistics compiled by Miss M. Hogg, published in an article, " Dependants on Women Wage-earners," *Economica*, No. 1, January 1921. The results of investigations by Mr. B. S. Rowntree and Mr. Frank D. Stuart were published in *The Responsibility of Women Workers for Dependants*, London, 1921. Variations in the results of these enquiries appear to be due largely to differences of definition and methods of tabulation.

six.[1]   The number with persons wholly dependent
upon them appears to be about one in twenty.

The small proportion of women workers who maintain dependants has had an important influence on
the fixing of basic wages.   As already stated, the
method often adopted in Australia, the United States,
and Canada for determining basic rates for women is
to fix the wage at an amount adequate for the maintenance of a woman entirely dependent on her earnings,
but not responsible for the support of others.   This
is a reasonable basis for the great majority of women
workers, and its application has often resulted in
increases in wages.   It serves to protect women who
are dependent on their earnings from the competition
of women receiving income from other sources, including wives largely maintained by their husbands
and daughters partially maintained by their fathers.
Such competition has been responsible for much
misery among women dependent on their own
earnings.   It was partly to prevent the harmful
consequences of this competition that the minimum
wage laws of the United States and Canada were
enacted.

On the other hand, a basic wage determined according to the needs of the worker alone is inadequate
for those with dependants.   A large proportion of

[1] The proportion appears to be nearer one in three if women
workers are regarded as responsible for the maintenance of
dependants in families where an adult man is working, but
whose earnings are inadequate to support the family.   (See
Miss Hogg's article.)

I

women workers with dependants are widows, maintaining young children. Also sickness, unemployment,
or incapacity owing to industrial accidents of the
husband are responsible for many other cases of
women with dependants. With the provision of
adequate widows' pensions, old age pensions, and
accident, sickness, and unemployment insurance
benefits, the number of women responsible for
the maintenance of others would be greatly
reduced.

In practice, while large numbers of men are responsible for the maintenance of families, they will strenu-
ously resist reductions of wages to a level below that
necessary for such maintenance. As the majority of
women are without dependants, large numbers will
be prepared to work for a wage adequate for their
own maintenance alone. This being so, minimum
wage fixing bodies would find it difficult to secure
for women a much higher basic wage. The fixing of
the basic wage for women workers in accordance
with their needs alone, without provision for
dependants, would not prevent the earning of higher
wages according to ability.

EQUAL PAY FOR EQUAL WORK.[1]

This principle is here considered only from the
point of view of the relation between the wages of

[1] In addition to references already given, mention may be
made of Professor F. Y. Edgeworth's Presidential Address to

men and women, although it is capable of much wider application, including, as indicated in the previous chapter, payment of the same rate of wage to all men of given grade irrespective of the number of their dependants. The point of view is here entirely different from that of the preceding section. The application of the living wage principle implies a consideration of needs. These should be taken into account when fixing basic minima. The State determines the standard, based on national productivity, below which its workers should not be allowed to fall. However, the employer will not continue to employ workers whose work is of less value than the wages paid. The consequences have been examined in an earlier chapter.

The relation between the basic wages of men and women, determined according to needs, will differ considerably, apart from the family allowance system. Above the basic minima fixed in part for humanitarian reasons, the principle of payment for work done should, as far as practicable, be adopted. This implies equal pay for equal work. Difficulties are, however, encountered in the application of this apparently simple principle. The chief difficulty is to determine what constitutes equal work. Where work is different

Section F of the British Association, Hull, 1922, on the subject " Equal Pay to Men and Women for Equal Work " (*Economic Journal*, December 1922). The conclusions of the present section correspond closely with those of Professor Edgeworth, and also, apart from family allowances, with those of Mrs. Sidney Webb (Minority Report, Cd. 135).

in kind there is no logical basis for determining equality.
Thus there is no such basis for deciding the relation
between the value of the work of a docker and that
of a dairymaid. For work different in kind the factor
which will determine the relation between wages
in different occupations is the reaction of demand
and supply. This factor operates to determine the
relation between wages in occupations in which men
only are employed and wages in women's occupations.
Over a large field of industry the relation is determined in this way, as the number of occupations in
which men and women are engaged on identical
work is comparatively small. Even in an industry
like the textile industry, in which both sexes are
employed in large numbers, there are many occupations which are predominantly men's, while others
are almost exclusively women's occupations. The
rougher or more dangerous tasks are undertaken by
men, and the lighter work by women.

However, there are certain occupations in which
men and women are employed in doing similar work.
In these, so far as equality of work can be determined,
wage rates should be equal for the two sexes. Equality
of work may be considered from three points of view.
Subjectively, work may be considered as the effort
exerted by the worker and the fatigue which this
involves. It is not generally possible to measure
work from the subjective point of view with any reasonable degree of accuracy. Objectively, the amount of
work done may be tested either by output or by the

value of the work to the employer.[1] In occupations for which piece rates of wages are fixed, the output test implies equality of piece rates for all workers, without distinction of sex, earnings varying according to output. But a given quantity of work done by different persons is not necessarily of equal value to the employer. Workers who produce a large number of units during a given period may be of greater value per unit of output to the employer than workers who produce less. This is especially true where overhead charges are high. The slow worker costs more per unit of output for interest on capital, rent, and management than does the quick worker. Therefore, if in a given piece-work occupation the average output of women during a week or other period is less than that of men, it might be considered reasonable to fix lower piece rates for women than for men so as to secure equality of value to the employer. It is preferable, however, if the nature of the work done by men and women is identical, that the same piece-work rates should apply without distinction of sex. A stimulus to a high rate of output could be provided by the payment of a higher piece rate for each unit produced beyond a given number, or by some form of premium bonus to workers attaining a given output. Such bonus or higher piece rate payment would apply equally to men and women.

[1] The subjective and the two objective aspects were examined by Mrs. Sidney Webb in her War Cabinet Committee Minority Report on Women in Industry (Cd. 135).

In the argument that to secure equality in value of work to the employer a lower piece rate should be fixed for the sex with the lower average output, it is overlooked that an employer is free to employ men and women in whatever proportions he finds the most satisfactory. If men have greater aptitude than women for a given occupation a large proportion of men will be employed, although a certain number of women may be able to secure employment. In other occupations women will predominate, although a certain number of men may be employed.

Similarly where men and women perform equal work in the same occupation at time rates, these should be the same for either sex. If in any trade men are generally more competent than women they will constitute the larger part of its personnel, although certain women specially suited to the trade may also be employed. The converse is equally true. The general effect of equality of rates of pay, whether on a time or piece basis, would be a distribution of men and women in the different occupations according to their efficiency at different kinds of work. In order that the process of distribution may work satisfactorily, artificial obstacles to the free entry of women into any occupation not obviously unsuitable should be broken down. In other words, there should be equality of opportunity.

The foregoing sections show that, for fixing basic minima below which no worker should fall, the most practicable plan, apart from the adoption of the family allowance system, is for the man's wage to be fixed in relation to a family of average size and the woman's wage in relation to her own requirements. The amounts should be determined according to the general productivity of industry, and not vary with the capacity of each separate trade. These basic rates should be applied as minima for unskilled men and women respectively, where the two sexes are engaged on work different in kind. If the work is identical in the case of ordinary unskilled occupations, men and women should be paid at the men's rate. For equal work in more highly paid employment the minimum rate should be the same for both sexes, the amount being determined according to the capacity of each separate industry. For unequal work above the basic minima the law of demand and supply in each occupation will determine within narrow limits the relation which the minimum wage authority can fix.

Addendum.

The following table is of interest as showing the relation between the wages of men and women in various countries. All the statistics, except those for the United States, are taken from official sources ; the United States figures are from the publications of the National Industrial Conference Board, an employers' organisation. The figures given are averages of the wages in a large number of industries in each country

RELATION IN VARIOUS COUNTRIES BETWEEN THE WAGES OF MEN AND WOMEN.

Country.	Nature of Statistics.	Date.	Average Wage.		Ratio of Women's to Men's Wages. Men's Wage=100.
			Men.	Women.	
Australia	Weekly rates	Sept.30, 1925	95s. 10d.	50s. 2d.	53
Denmark	Hourly earnings	4th qr., 1925	1·67 crowns	0·97 crowns	58
France	Daily rates	Oct. 1924	22 frs.	11·36 frs.	52
Great Britain ..	Trade Board hourly minima	Jan. 1, 1926	1s. 0½d.	0s. 7d.	56
Germany (Textiles)— Spinners and Weavers	Weekly rates	Feb. 1925	26·59 R.Mks.	21·46 R.Mks.	81
Helpers	Do.	Do.	22·22 R.Mks.	16·42 R.Mks.	74
India (Bombay)— Cotton Mill Workers	Full-time daily earnings	Aug. 1923	1·36 Rs.	0·72 Rs.	53
Sweden	Hourly earnings	1924	1·14 crowns	0·70 crowns	61
United States ..	Weekly earn- ings	June 1925	28·98 $	16·95 $	59
New York State ..	Weekly earn- ings	April 1926	32·46 $	18·09 $	56
Massachusetts ..	Weekly earn- ings	May 1926	29·19 $	16·62 $	57

except Germany and India, for which recent data are available for the textile industry only. In many countries the ratio between the wages of men and women in the textile industry is not representative of the general relation, there being less inequality in that industry than in most other important industries. Thus, in Massachusetts, whereas the general ratio in May 1926 shown in the table was males = 100, females = 57, in the cotton industry the ratio was males = 100, females = 76, and in the woollen and worsted industry, males = 100, females = 75.

The relation shown, that the wages of women are generally about 50 to 60 per cent. of those of men, has little bearing on the question as to the practicability of applying the principle of equal pay for equal work in those occupations in which men and women are employed on similar work. The statistics include large numbers of occupations in which men and women are employed on different work. They indicate the effects of all the factors which result in large numbers of women doing low-paid work.

CHAPTER IX

WAGES BELOW THE GENERAL MINIMUM

This chapter deals with the problem of fixing special rates for workers who are below the normal level of efficiency, and also for adult learners and juveniles. Reference is made to methods of preventing the abuses and hardships which may follow the fixing of special wages below the ordinary minimum for these groups of workers.

SUB-STANDARD WORKERS.

Efficiency below the average may be the result of infirmity or physical injury. There is also the case of the "slow worker" who, "while not subject to any infirmity or physical injury, is yet incapable, owing to some constitutional defect, or to age, or some other cause, of earning the minimum fixed for the ordinary worker of his class."[1]

Owing to the lower efficiency of sub-standard workers, the application to them of a minimum time wage appropriate to the general body of workers would result in their unemployment. The alternative is to grant them permission to work at a lower rate than the ordinary minimum. Most minimum wage laws provide for the adoption of this course. There

[1] Report of the Cave Committee, Cd. 1645, p. 34.

are advantages in not drawing too rigidly the line separating the worker from the unemployable. If allowance is made for their lesser productivity, substandard workers will be able to contribute to the national dividend, while unemployment and the necessity for full maintenance out of public funds will be avoided. In so far, however, as the general minimum fixed for ordinary workers represents the minimum standard of living considered reasonable according to the general productivity of industry, the fixing of a lower rate implies that although the evils of unemployment are avoided, those due to an inferior standard are encountered. In order to prevent misery the issue of permits to work for rates below the general minimum should be accompanied by the right to State assistance to make up the difference.

The granting of exceptions from the general minimum introduces the risk of employers claiming that a considerable number of their workers are below the average in efficiency. Clearly the issue of permits must be strictly controlled if the value of the general minimum is to be preserved.

The number of workers with a definite infirmity or injury is limited. In their case there is little danger of an excessive number of exemptions being granted. The requirement of a doctor's certificate prior to issuing the permit is generally a sufficient safeguard against abuse. Also the granting of exemptions to workers over a given age involves little danger. There may be considerable abuse, however, in the case of "slow workers." This is largely avoided by the practice adopted in certain countries of fixing the proportion between the number of exempted workers and the total number of workers in any establishment. Often exemptions are granted only for a limited period, after which each case is reconsidered.

In the United States persons incompetent by reason of age or disability due to physical or mental defect to earn the minimum wage fixed for ordinary workers may be given licences permitting their employment at lower rates.[1] In Colorado, Minnesota, and Texas, licences to work at rates below the general minimum for ordinary workers may be given to not more than one-tenth of the workers in any establishment. In Texas and in California, where the number of licences is also regulated, exemptions are issued for periods of six months only, after which, unless renewed, ordinary rates apply.

The Canadian Provinces have applied measures similar to those in the United States. The system of licences for " handicapped " or " physically defective " workers is adopted. Generally the number of licences issued is small, and in some cases a definite limit is fixed to the total which may be granted. Thus in British Columbia the number of licences for physically defective workers, and also for apprentices, shall not exceed one-seventh of the total number of workers

---

[1] United States Bureau of Labor Statistics, Bulletin, No. 285, *Minimum Wage Laws of the United States : Construction and Operation*, p. 21.

in any establishment.[1] Generally only in the case of permanent disablement is a permit granted for an indefinite period.

In Great Britain the Trade Boards Acts provide for the issue of permits of exemption to persons affected by an infirmity or physical injury, but not to those who from age or any other cause are incapable of earning the minimum rate. In 1922 the Cave Committee recommended that exemptions should be granted to the latter class also, and, in practice, permits are issued now in cases of infirmity due to age as well as to physical or mental defects. Many Boards have set up small committees charged with the special task of dealing with permits. No limit is fixed to the number of exemptions which may be granted, but, in practice, few permits are given, the total number at the end of 1925 being 2,320.[2] Exemption may be granted for a given period, often twelve months, or for an indefinite period. In various Australian States provision is made for the issue of exemption licences to handicapped and aged workers.

So far, attention has been directed to the question of granting exemption from minimum *time* rates

[1] This limitation is fixed only by the law applying to female workers. The Male Minimum Wage Act passed in 1925 does not impose a limit, although it confers on the Board which fixes the minimum rates the power to do so.

[2] *Report of the Ministry of Labour for the Year 1925* (Cd. 2763). The small number is, in part, due to the fact that in certain trades minimum piece rates are fixed, and permits are not issued unless the minimum piece rate is coupled with a guaranteed time minimum.

fixed for ordinary workers. A special case arises with regard to piece rates. Often a specified amount per day or per week is guaranteed as a minimum time rate and paid to all piece-workers whether they earn it or not. In such cases it is necessary to provide for the granting of exemption permits to handicapped workers on the lines already indicated. Otherwise workers unable to earn the guaranteed time rate would be faced with unemployment, and there would be danger of excessive strain on workers who found difficulty in reaching the guaranteed minimum.

In some cases a minimum time rate is not guaranteed to piece-workers. If each employer fixes his own piece rates, the minimum wage fixing authority may provide that a given proportion of the piece-workers in any establishment shall be able to earn not less than a certain amount per day or per week. Such a provision is at once a safeguard as to the fairness of the piece rates and a means of allowing automatic exemption to a certain proportion of workers. For example, already in the early days of the British Trade Boards the practice was adopted in the tailoring and paper box making industries of providing that in any establishment not less than 85 per cent. of the workers on piece rates must, on an average, earn not less than a fixed minimum day wage.[1] The Ontario

[1] See R. H. Tawney, *Minimum Rates in the Tailoring Industry*, pp. 50-1, and M. E. Buckley, *Minimum Rates in the Box-making Industry*, pp. 21-2. Even with such a practice as that under consideration it is still open to employers, as Mr. Tawney points out, to discharge their worst

Minimum Wage Board adopts this system, the proportion being 80 per cent. In California the Minimum Wage Commission has fixed the proportion at 66⅔ per cent.[1] Other Wage Boards and Commissions have adopted this method of securing reasonable piece rates. By fixing the proportion of workers who are to earn a given sum per day at 85 per cent., 80 per cent., or 66⅔ per cent., exemption is " granted " to 15 per cent., 20 per cent., or 33⅓ per cent. respectively of workers below the level of efficiency of ordinary workers.

ADULT LEARNERS AND JUVENILES.[2]

The problem of fixing special rates for adult learners and juveniles presents less difficulty in some respects than in the case of sub-standard workers. The latter generally constitute a permanent problem, whereas workers, engage more efficient workers instead, and then fix piece rates below those which would have been necessary to enable 85 per cent. of their original workpeople to earn the minimum time rate. This danger of cutting the piece rate may be avoided, in part, by not accepting as reasonable without question the piece rate of an employer who has dismissed a considerable number of his slow workers immediately prior to fixing the rate.

[1] Commons and Andrews, *Principles of Labour Legislation.*

[2] Juveniles may be either young workers who are given no special facilities for learning the trade, learners who are given such facilities, or apprentices who, in addition to being given opportunities for learning the trade, are bound by written contract to serve for a specified number of years. Generally the first category receives higher rates than the other two, while lower minima are sometimes fixed for apprentices than for learners of the same age.

the former require lower rates for the period of training only. There are, however, special difficulties. Thus, for adult learners, an employer, if free to do so, may fix an unduly long period for learning the trade, and thus obtain work at low rates from fairly experienced workers. In trades requiring little skill an employer may take advantage of the lower rates for juveniles, and employ them in large numbers until they become entitled to the wages of adults. They are then discharged and their places taken by other workers at beginners' rates, the industry becoming a blind alley.

In the case of adult learners, Minimum Wage Boards generally fix the period during which such workers shall be regarded as inexperienced and paid at lower rates. The length of time usually varies according to the nature of the occupation, ranging from three months in occupations where the work is easily learned, to eighteen months where the trade is more difficult. Thus in Saskatchewan, workers in hotels, restaurants, and refreshment-rooms are regarded as inexperienced during their first three months, after which they must be paid the ordinary minimum wage. In the case of workers in laundries and factories a training period of eighteen months is recognised. Many Boards in different countries provide that, if the period of training is considerable, the wages of inexperienced adults shall be increased by successive stages as training proceeds. Thus the Ontario Minimum Wage Board, in an Order which came into effect on October 1st, 1924 governing the conditions of female workers in the tobacco trades, provides that inexperienced women in Toronto shall receive not less than 10 dollars per week for the first six months, and 11 dollars per week for the second six months, after which they become entitled to the rate of 12 dollars 50 cents per week for experienced women.

In addition to limiting the period during which lower rates may be paid to adult learners, in some countries the number of such learners is also limited, licences being issued allowing them to work at special rates. The Canadian Minimum Wage Boards have this power of limitation, but the proportion of learners to experienced workers varies from one Province to another. Generally the proportion includes both adult learners and juveniles, although in British Columbia licences are required only for inexperienced workers of eighteen years of age and over. The Ontario Minimum Wage Board limits the number of inexperienced adult women and young girls to one-half of the total female working force.[1] In Manitoba the proportion is 25 per cent. The Orders of the Alberta Board provide that not more than 20 per cent. of the entire female working staff shall be apprentices or learners. Certain Minimum Wage Commissions in the United States are empowered to limit the number of learners. Similar provisions are applied in Australia. The British Trade Boards impose no limits.

[1] Neither the number of inexperienced adult women nor the number of young girls shall exceed one-third of the total female working force.

The rates for juveniles are generally fixed on the
basis of age or experience, or a combination of both.[1]
The age basis, according to which wages advance by
stages, for example, every six or twelve months
during the period from fourteen years to the adult
age, has certain disadvantages.   There is little incentive
for the worker to learn the trade quickly.   No automatic scale provides this incentive.   Also juveniles
older than those who enter the industry at the bottom
of the scale will find difficulty in obtaining employment.   The age basis has been adopted by certain
boards in Great Britain and Australia.   In these
countries, however, and also in Canada and the United
States, rates for juveniles are more often fixed on the
basis of experience.   Thus the Ontario Minimum
Wage Board in a number of its Orders prescribes
that the minimum weekly rate for girls under eighteen
years of age in Toronto shall be :—

	Dollars.
First six months	8
Second six months	9
Third six months	10
Subsequently, the experienced workers' rate	12½

Such a method removes part of the difficulty with
regard to late entrants.   It suffers from the defect
that children entering the occupation at the school-
leaving age, e.g. fourteen years, will be earning higher
wages than those who join the trade a year or two
later, although the latter may learn more quickly,

[1] Rates for juvenile workers are sometimes varied according
to sex.   Differences based on occupation are rarely made.

and may, on account of their age, be of greater value to the employer. This difficulty is avoided in part by establishing a scale based on age and experience combined. The following example of such a scale is taken from the wage rates fixed by the British Lace Finishing Trade Board.

MINIMUM WEEKLY RATES OF WAGES OF FEMALE LEARNERS WORKING ON FRAME CLIPPING IN THE LACE FINISHING INDUSTRY.[1]

Learners commencing at—	Period of Service.		
	First Six Months.	Second Six Months.	Second Year.
	s. d.	s. d.	s. d.
Under 15 years of age ..	8 0	9 0	12 0
15 and under 16 years of age	9 0	12 0	16 0
16 and under 17 years of age	10 0	14 0	19 0
17 and under 18 years of age	10 0	16 0	—

This method of combining age and experience has been adopted by a number of Trade Boards in Great Britain, and also by Wage Boards in Australia, e.g. in Victoria. Many variations are found both in periods of service and in differences of age.

As in the case of adult learners, it is often provided that juveniles must have licences to work at lower rates, and the number of workers with licences in any

[1] The rates, which came into operation on April 5th, 1922, are for a week of forty-eight hours.

establishment is limited to a given proportion of the
total number of workers in the establishment.   Thus
in Victoria many Trade Boards provide that the
proportion shall be one apprentice and one improver
to every three, or fraction of three, adult workers.[1]

[1] An improver is generally a learner under twenty-one
years of age.

CHAPTER X

MACHINERY FOR FIXING MINIMUM WAGES

THE chief means by which minimum rates of wages may be fixed are :—

(1) Trade Boards ;
(2) Central Commissions ;
(3) Arbitration Courts ;
(4) Direct legal enactment ;
(5) General application of collective agreements.

In the following sections each of these methods is examined. It is shown that the Trade Board system is of value where wages are to be fixed independently according to the conditions of each separate industry. Where wages in the different industries are to be determined according to a common policy, or where a national minimum is to be fixed, a Central Commission is necessary. Arbitration Courts are set up where the purpose is to prevent industrial disputes. Minimum wages fixed by direct legal enactment are generally too rigid to meet the requirements of varying economic conditions. The extension of collective agreements reached by some of the employers and workers in a trade to apply to the whole trade is a useful supplement to other methods of fixing minimum wages.

TRADE BOARDS.

The machinery which has been most frequently adopted for fixing minimum wages is Trade Boards. The essential feature of a Trade Board is that it is concerned solely with wages, and other conditions of labour, in the industry in which it is set up.[1] This system has been applied in Great Britain, in Victoria, Tasmania, and, in conjunction with Arbitration Courts, in other States of the Commonwealth of Australia. Trade Boards have also been set up in certain countries of continental Europe—France, Germany, Austria, Czechoslovakia, Norway—and in the Argentine Republic.

A Trade Board consists of an equal number of representatives of employers and workers, together with disinterested persons. In Austria boards consist of at least nine members, one-third representing the employers, one-third the workers, the remaining third being independent experts. In Great Britain the boards vary in size in rough proportion to the number of workers in the trade. The smallest board consists of 15 persons, while the largest has about 50 members. At the end of 1924 the total membership of the 43 boards then in existence in Great Britain was 1,659, or an average membership of nearly 40 ; the number of independent persons on any board is, in practice, limited to three. In Australia boards vary in size

---

[1] Difficulties are often encountered in defining the limits of the industry covered by any board.

according to industry and State. The membership usually ranges from 5 to 11 persons, only one of whom is disinterested.

Trade Boards may be constituted either for a given district only or for the country as a whole. There are disadvantages in setting up separate boards for the same trade in different districts. The limits of districts are often difficult of definition. Great diversity of rates may prevail unless there is a central authority with power to ensure reasonable uniformity of action by the district boards. The French Home-work Act of 1915 is an example of a law permitting the maximum of decentralisation. Independent wage boards are set up in each department, and these fix wages for the trades covered. There is practically no co-ordination between the different boards. If objection is raised to the rate fixed by any board, the matter is referred to a central board in Paris, but the main object of this central board appears to be to secure agreement for the department concerned, rather than to bring about any uniformity between the rates fixed in different departments. In consequence of the system of local boards, and the lack of co-ordination between them, great diversity of rates has resulted. In some departments the minimum rates have been revised regularly as provided by the law. In others they have remained unchanged since 1916, 1917, or 1918, and are totally ineffective in view of the changes that have taken place in the cost of living. Even where revisions have been simultaneous in various departments, the differences in rates are great. Thus in the second quarter of 1925 the minimum rate for " lingerie " work in the Meurthe-et-Moselle Department was fixed at 1·50 francs per hour, while in the neighbouring Vosges Department the minimum fixed at almost the same date was only 75 centimes.[1] Such differences are evidently greater than would be warranted by differences in economic conditions, including the cost of living.

In certain countries in which minimum rates are fixed on a district basis, attempts are made to secure co-ordination. Thus in Germany, under the Homework Act of 1923, wage boards are normally appointed for given districts only.[2] In order, however, to avoid unfair competition, and to prevent the tendency of workers to migrate from one district to another owing to lack of uniformity in the rates fixed in different districts, provision is made as occasion arises for the convocation of joint boards to act for several districts together.

Co-ordination is greater in countries where the rates fixed by the board in any locality are subject to confirmation by a central authority. Thus in Norway the rates fixed for homeworkers by a local board are not operative until confirmed by a Central Homework Council, which has also power to amend the rates, or to refer them back to the local board for reconsideration.

[1] *Bulletin du Ministère du Travail*, July–August–September 1925 ; article on the application of the Homework Act.

[2] For the application of the Homework Act, see an article in the *Reichsarbeitsblatt*, December 9th, 1926.

The highest degree of co-ordination between minimum rates fixed for workers in a given trade in different
districts is secured by the system widely adopted in
Great Britain, Victoria, and Tasmania, and for homework trades in Austria and Czechoslovakia. Wages are
often fixed in different industries or branches by Trade
Boards covering the whole country. Provision is
usually made for these boards to set up District Committees where necessary to advise them as to rates
suitable for any district.[1] Thus a national Trade
Board may either fix uniform rates in all districts,
or may fix separate rates in different districts. Which-
ever course it takes, the board is in a position to ensure
co-ordination between rates in different parts of the
country.

The chief difficulty of a National Trade Board when
fixing district rates is that of defining the limits of
the different districts. The difficulty is less in the
case of trades having a local market than where the
market is national or international. In the latter
case uniform rates for all districts are generally satisfactory, apart from wide differences in the cost of
living. In Great Britain, Trade Boards usually fix
uniform minima for the whole country. Where more
than one scale is fixed the differences between the
rates are usually small. In four or‚ five trades, one
board fixes rates for England and Wales while there is

[1] In Great Britain at the end of 1924 only six Trade Boards
had set up District Committees, the number of these being
thirty-four.

a separate board for Scotland. The Laundry Trade Board fixes a lower rate for experienced female workers in Cornwall and the North of Scotland than that for the rest of Great Britain. In the Milk Distributive Trade there are four different minima, three applicable to different parts of England and Wales according to population, and the fourth to Scotland.[1] In certain countries less industrially homogeneous than Great Britain greater district variation in rates is found.

It has been seen that co-ordination between rates fixed for the same trade in different districts is most effectively secured if one Trade Board, acting for the whole country, fixes the rates for all districts. This system, however, suffers from the defect that separate boards are set up for each trade. These boards are independent of one another, and action taken in similar circumstances may vary considerably from one board to another. Some method of co-ordination between different Trade Boards is therefore necessary. In certain countries, for example in Great Britain, Norway, Austria, and Czechoslovakia, this is to some extent ensured by making the rates fixed by any board subject to confirmation by a central authority, whether Government Department or specially constituted central body.[2] This authority has power to refer back

---

[1] *Report of the Minister of Labour for the Year 1925* (Cd. 2736) gives the Trade Board minimum rates in force on December 31st, 1925.

[2] The Department or other central body can also undertake the task of inspection and enforcement more appropriately than the separate boards.

for further consideration the rates fixed by a board. In Victoria appeals against rates fixed by a board may be made to the Court of Industrial Appeals, which has power to modify the decisions. The Court is thus able to exercise a co-ordinating influence. In New South Wales, South Australia, and Queensland appeals from determinations of boards may be made to the Arbitration Courts.[1]

Other means exist for co-ordinating the work of different Trade Boards. Thus in Great Britain a number of employers' and workers' representatives, and also of independent members, sit on more than one board. This involves the representation of employers and workers to some extent by persons outside the trade for which the board has been set up ; however, the advantages of co-ordination outweigh any disadvantage due to lack of experience in the trade. In New South Wales a certain degree of co-ordination is secured by the provision that the same chairman shall preside over a number of boards in allied trades.

CENTRAL COMMISSIONS.

In the previous section reference has been made to certain methods of co-ordinating the work of Trade Boards. Since, however, rates of wages are fixed

---

[1] In certain States it is asserted that the authority of boards is weakened by the system of appeal, as employers or workers are less anxious to secure determinations of the boards than if their decisions were final.

by independent boards, complete co-ordination cannot be effected. Under the Central Commission system, rates in different industries are fixed by a single authority, the greatest possible co-ordination thus being secured. This system has been adopted in certain States in Australia and in most of the States or Provinces of the United States and Canada which have passed minimum wage laws.

The Commission may fix different rates for each industry or may determine a general minimum applicable to all industries. The former method has been adopted in the United States and in Canada. The latter, which implies the fixing of a national minimum wage, has been applied on a wide scale in Australia and New Zealand.

In the United States and Canada Commissions or minimum wage boards generally consist of three or five members only. Some Commissions are composed entirely of disinterested persons. Others must include a representative of the employers and a representative of the workers. Often at least one of the members of the Commission must be a woman. In certain cases the Commissioner of Labour, or other similar official, is a member and acts as chairman. Commissioners are usually appointed for a fixed period, which varies in different States or Provinces from two to six years.

As, in the United States and Canada, different rates are fixed for each industry, the conditions of each must be taken into consideration. The Commission, however, cannot know these special conditions in any detail. Therefore it generally either sets up permanent boards in each industry, consisting of representatives of employers and workers, or calls together special conferences of employers and workers. These Trade Boards or Trade Conferences advise the Commission as to the rates to be fixed in the trade concerned. During meetings of such advisory boards or conferences, members of the Commission, and especially its chairman, endeavour to secure satisfactory agreements, and in doing so act as conciliators much in the same way as do the independent members of Trade Boards. In co-ordinating rates in different industries the functions of a Central Commission correspond closely with those performed under the Trade Board system by the Government Department or other central authority. In practice, therefore, the Commission system may closely resemble that of Trade Boards. However, as already indicated, there is an essential difference between the two systems. Under the Trade Board system, rates for different trades are fixed by independent boards, while under the Commission system they are fixed by one central authority.

Although, in the United States and Canada, Commissions often fix different minimum rates for different industries, the variations are generally small. This is due largely to the adoption of the cost of living as basis for the rates. Variations are due mainly to differences in the nature of the work in different

industries.   Usually the minimum fixed for any trade
applies throughout the trade.   In some States or
Provinces, however, minima varying according to
district are fixed.   Thus in Minnesota and Wisconsin
different rates have been fixed for workers in cities
with 5,000 or more inhabitants, from those in towns
with fewer inhabitants.   In Kansas and North Dakota
variations according to size of town are also made for
workers in certain trades, e.g. telephone operators.
The Ontario Minimum Wage Board fixes different
minima in different towns, according to their population.   Four   groups   of   towns   are   distinguished.
According to Orders which came into force in September or October 1924, the minimum weekly rates
of experienced women workers in a large number of
trades were :—

	Dollars.
City of Toronto	12·50
Other cities of 30,000 population and over	11·50
Cities and towns between 5,000 and 30,000 population	11·00
Towns below 5,000 population, and rural districts ..	10·00

On the other hand, in Saskatchewan and British
Columbia a single minimum rate for experienced
workers in any one industry is applicable throughout
the Province.   To a considerable extent the minimum
rates fixed for experienced workers in different Provinces in Canada vary within the narrow limits of
12½ to 14 or 15 dollars per week, according to industry.
In certain States in the United States the range is
greater.

In Australia and New Zealand the greatest progress

has been made towards uniformity of minimum rates in different industries and districts. In New South Wales an Industrial Commission consisting of three members is charged with the duty of declaring from time to time the amount of a living wage for adult males and females. Since 1926 the Commission is no longer empowered to make separate declarations for workers in urban and rural areas, but is required to fix minima of State-wide application. In addition to these general declarations, the Commission makes awards in cases of dispute. In South Australia the Board of Industry, which consists of a president with four commissioners, two of whom represent the employers and two the workers, is also required to declare the amount of a living wage. In Queensland the Board of Trade and Arbitration, in addition to dealing with cases of dispute, has powers of a general character, including that of making declarations as to the cost of living and the minimum rates of wages to be paid to persons of either sex. Thus the Board performs the functions both of an Arbitration Court and of a Central Commission for the purpose of fixing basic wages applicable to all industries. In Western Australia the Industrial Arbitration Court is required not only to make awards in cases of dispute, but to declare basic wages of general application. Similarly in New Zealand, since 1919, the Arbitration Court has declared minimum wage rates applicable to practically all industries. It fixes three separate minima, for skilled, semi-skilled, and unskilled workers respectively, and these rates apply throughout the country.[1] The maximum degree of wage standardisation is thus attained. In all these States the declarations fix basic minima of general application either in the State as a whole or in a defined area thereof. This is a logical outcome of the acceptance of the living wage principle.

As has been indicated, greater co-ordination is possible under a Central Commission than under Trade Boards. The setting up of Trade Boards in low-paid unorganised industries may be the first step in effecting improvements in wages, but the establishment of machinery of the Central Commission type is essential if progress is to be made towards a general minimum wage applicable to all industries.

ARBITRATION COURTS.

The Arbitration Court system is adopted where the main object is to settle disputes and to facilitate the establishment of industrial peace. Arbitration may be either voluntary or compulsory. Where resort to arbitration is voluntary, the machinery is put into operation and wages fixed only on request of the parties to a dispute. As the Court is not entitled to take the initiative there is no real interference with freedom of contract. The disputing parties merely undertake to accept the findings of a Court to which

[1] Since 1923 the Court has declared that it may award rates below the general minima in any industry where exceptional circumstances warrant such a decision.

they have agreed to submit their differences. Where arbitration is compulsory the State definitely interferes with freedom of contract, and undertakes, in certain cases, to regulate wages and other conditions of labour. In the present study compulsory arbitration only is considered.

The essential function of an Arbitration Court is to make awards in cases of dispute only. A Court thus differs from a Trade Board or a Central Commission, which may fix minimum rates at any time, whether a dispute has arisen or not.[1] Also rates fixed by a Court are generally not merely minimum, but also maximum rates. Employers may not pay less than the rates fixed, while workers may not strike for more.

Since disputes may arise in any industry or occupation, an Arbitration Court may be called upon to fix wages in a large number of different industries. In this it resembles the Central Commission, and differs from Trade Boards. The Court has thus no technical knowledge of the industries with which it deals. It must, however, consider the reaction of any award fixing wages for workers in a given industry on workers in other industries. The Court is obliged, therefore, to adopt general principles which it can apply to all cases of a similar character.

[1] Where, as in Queensland, New South Wales, Western Australia, and New Zealand, an Arbitration Court also fixes basic minima without reference to a dispute, it is performing the function of a Central Commission in addition to that of a Court.

The Arbitration Court system is most highly developed in New Zealand and Australia. In these countries Courts consist either of a president, with or without one or more deputies or additional judges, appointed from among persons of given legal standing, or of a president, together with one or two members recommended by employers' organisations and an equal number recommended by workers' organisations. The Australian Commonwealth Court and the State Courts of Queensland and South Australia are constituted in the former manner, while in Western Australia, New South Wales, and New Zealand membership of the Court is determined on the latter plan. In certain States, e.g. New South Wales and Western Australia, the Court may appoint one or two assessors from each side of a dispute to sit with the Court to advise it. Similarly the Australian Commonwealth Arbitration Court has power to appoint one assessor from each side for advisory purposes. Members of Courts are usually appointed for a given period of years, subject to good behaviour, and are eligible for reappointment for further periods.

When a dispute is brought before an Arbitration Court, evidence is presented both from the employers' and the workers' side. Often counsel are employed to present the cases. After the hearing the Court makes an award, which may be binding only on parties to the dispute. However, the fact that certain rates of wages have been fixed in an award has an indirect influence on the wages of similar groups of workers. It is recognised that the Court would probably make similar awards if other cases in which the same conditions prevailed were brought before it. Certain Arbitration Courts, for example those in New Zealand and South Australia, have power to extend the application of an award to all employers and workers in the industry concerned, either in a given district or in the State as a whole.

DIRECT LEGAL ENACTMENT.

This method is comparatively rare. One reason for its application has been to prevent the employment of young learners and apprentices without a wage, under the pretence of teaching a trade. Wages fixed for this purpose are low. Thus a rate of 2s. 6d. per week has been fixed in Victoria, and of 4s. per week in South Australia. In Queensland, Tasmania, and New Zealand rates of 4s. to 7s. 6d. per week have been fixed for the first year, with specified increases according to length of service.

This method has also been adopted for the prevention of sweating among adult workers. It has been used for this purpose for female workers in the United States—in Arizona, Arkansas,[1] Porto Rico, South Dakota, and Utah—and in South America for

[1] In Arkansas, although minimum rates for experienced and inexperienced female workers have been fixed by statute, an Industrial Welfare Commission has been set up with power to raise or lower the statutory minima.

agricultural workers in Uruguay. In Arizona the statutory minimum wage for female workers is $16 per week. In Porto Rico the minimum wage for female workers under eighteen years of age is $4 per week, and for those over eighteen, $6 per week. In South Dakota the minimum for women and girls over fourteen years of age, excluding apprentices, is $12 per week. In Utah the rate fixed for experienced female workers over eighteen years of age is $1·25 per day, lower minima being fixed for workers under eighteen, for learners and apprentices. In Uruguay the minimum wage of rural labourers between eighteen and fifty-five years of age engaged in agriculture or in stock-raising on large estates is 80 centesimos per day, together with sanitary housing accommodation and sufficient food, or a money equivalent. Lower minima are fixed for workers on smaller farms, and also for workers between sixteen and eighteen years and over fifty-five years of age.

The fixing by statute of minimum wages for adult workers is open to various objections. In most countries, until the wages of unskilled workers in different industries have become more standardised by the action of Trade Boards or Central Commissions, a minimum rate fixed by direct legal enactment can be of little value. So long as the wage rates of the lowest paid groups of workers in different industries differ considerably, any statutory minimum which could be fixed would be so low that it would benefit only a small number of workers in a few of the lowest paid industries. To fix a higher rate would cause considerable unemployment.

Even when the wages of unskilled workers are more standardised than at present, the method of fixing minimum rates by direct statutory enactment would be unsatisfactory. A legislative assembly is unsuited to the task of examining the detailed information on which the minimum rates would be based. Political influences would interfere with the fixing of the wage warranted by economic conditions. Also legislative processes are generally too slow to permit of the adjustment necessary as economic conditions change.

GENERAL APPLICATION OF COLLECTIVE AGREEMENTS.

Prevention of unfair competition between employers may be secured to a greater or less extent by collective agreement. Certain methods of determining minimum wages closely resemble the processes of collective bargaining, and there may be little difference in practice between a wage rate fixed by a Trade Board after agreement between the employers and workers represented on it, and a wage rate fixed by collective agreement. One essential difference is that wage rates fixed by a Trade Board apply to all workers in the industry or occupation covered, whereas those fixed by collective agreement are binding only on the parties to the agreement. The degree of standardisation of wage rates by means of collective agreements varies therefore with the size of the organistions concluding them.[1]   A further difference between Trade Board minima and rates fixed by collective agreements is that the former are legally binding while the latter may not be so.[2]

In a number of countries legislation has been adopted under which the provisions of collective agreements may be declared legally binding, not only on the parties to the agreement, but on all engaged in similar work.   In most cases the terms of agreement are only made of general application if the agreement covers a large proportion of all employers and workers in the industry.   In the present section reference is made to various laws applying the system.   For the purpose of illustration, mention is made both of laws by which State-established machinery has compulsory powers to extend an agreement, and of laws by which extension is made only on request by the parties concerned.

The generalisation of collective agreements is established by laws in certain States in Australia, and also in Germany, Austria, and South Africa ; while proposals with the object of introducing the system have been made in Great Britain and other countries. In New South Wales the principle of the " common

---

[1] The degree of standardisation also depends on the relation between the rates fixed in the agreements and the rates actually paid.   Often the agreed rates are minima, and most workers are paid at higher rates.

[2] In some countries, e.g. Austria and Germany, collective agreements are legally binding on the parties concerned, while in other countries, e.g. Great Britain, they are not so.

rule," or extension of an agreement, was applied by legislation as early as 1901, and has been adopted also in other States, e.g. South Australia and Queensland. In Germany the Federal Ministry of Labour may declare a collective agreement binding upon the whole of an industry within a given area, if it is of outstanding importance in that industry and area.[1] This system appears to have worked successfully, a large number of collective agreements having been declared of general application. Certain groups of workers, especially miners, have raised objections on the grounds that unorganised workers make no contribution to the Trade Unions, the members of which are fighting for benefits which accrue, not only to themselves, but also to those who have taken no part in the struggle.[2]

In Austria the Conciliation Boards set up under the Act of December 18th, 1919, may declare a collective agreement which has acquired dominant importance "to be binding as a whole or as regards particular

[1] This power was conferred by Section 2 of the Order, dated December 23rd, 1918, relating to collective agreements, committees of workers and employers, and conciliation in labour disputes. Such a declaration can be made only on the request of the signatory parties or of any organisation whose members would be affected. The Ministry of Labour is quite free to accede to, or refuse, the request. For the text of the Order see *Bulletin des Internationalen Arbeitsamts* (German edition), vol. XVII, page 182.

[2] *International Labour Review*, October 1922, "The Law of Collective Bargaining in Germany," by Dr. Fritz Sitzler. Little information is available for other countries as to the results of applying the " common rule."

provisions, even outside its field of operation, in respect of conditions of work fundamentally similar to those regulated by the collective agreement." [1] When such a declaration has been made, individual agreements shall be valid only if they are more favourable to the worker than the provisions made general by the declaration. However, if collective agreements not in conformity with the provisions of a declaration are concluded, they shall prevail over the declaration.

Somewhat similarly in South Africa, in the Act passed in 1924, providing for the prevention and settlement of industrial disputes by the creation of Joint Industrial Councils or of Conciliation Boards, it is stipulated that, where an Industrial Council or Conciliation Board lays down conditions for part of an industry, the Minister of Mines and Industries may, if he is satisfied that the parties on the Council or Board are sufficiently representative of the industry concerned, extend the finding to the whole industry. [2]

In Great Britain certain proposals for the generalisation of collective agreements have been discussed, but so far they have received no application. The first proposal on these lines was that made by the

[1] International Labour Office, Geneva, Legislative Series, 1920, Aus. 22, Act of December 18th, 1919, respecting the establishment of Conciliation Boards and respecting collective agreements. The Commissions set up under the Austrian Homework Act of December 1918 have also power to extend the sphere of operation of a collective agreement.

[2] International Labour Office, *Industrial and Labour Information*, vol. X, No. 13. The Act covers all industries, trades, and undertakings, except agriculture and farming.

Industrial Council set up after the coal strike in 1911. It was discussed by the Trade Union Congress, and rejected, largely owing to the opposition of the stronger unions. A second proposal was that embodied in a Bill called the "Industrial Councils Bill, 1923," the object of which was to give the Minister of Labour power to make binding upon the whole of any industry, on application by the Joint Industrial Council concerned, any wages awards or agreements as to hours and conditions made or confirmed by such Councils. With a view to safeguarding the rights of minorities, the Bill provided that not only must any such application be approved by the majority of each side of the Council, but where 10 per cent. of the industry object to the proposal, that 10 per cent. minority shall have the right to appeal to an independent tribunal. No progress has been made with the proposal. However, since the war, Trade Union opinion in Great Britain appears to be more favourable to the system.

The system of extending the provisions of collective agreements has the advantage that no elaborate or costly machinery for fixing wages need be set up ; also, since a large number of employers and workers in the industry have already voluntarily agreed to the wage rates, their extension to the remainder of the industry should cause little difficulty. Again, by this system the wages of different categories of workers with various degrees of skill may be readily fixed. On the other hand, the system suffers from the defect that the wage rate fixed by an agreement, especially where the workers' unions are weak, may be inadequate if considered in relation to the capacity of industry in general to pay. Also, as indicated above, the system may be opposed by Trade Unions on the ground that since workers who are not members of a union may, without effort on their part, benefit from the struggle of others, they will feel no necessity to join a workers' organisation, while those who are members may be tempted to withdraw. In Great Britain the more powerful unions feared, at least before the war, that the adoption of the system would tend towards the introduction of compulsory arbitration, to which they were strongly opposed.[1]

The advantages of the system, however, outweigh the disadvantages. The danger to Trade Unionism does not seem serious, and is more than balanced by compensating gains. Competition of employers not covered by an agreement and paying less than the agreed rates often endangers the maintenance of those rates. Also, attempts by Trade Unions to increase wages are rendered difficult if there exists a considerable volume of labour working at less than the agreed rates. The generalisation of agreed rates, by preventing undercutting, is of advantage to organisations both of employers and workers.

The system may be regarded as of value to supple-

[1] See an article by J. J. Mallon, " The Collapse of Wages. Is State Regulation Desirable ? " published in the *Manchester Guardian Commercial*, Reconstruction in Europe Series, Section 9.

ment State machinery for fixing minimum wages for the lowest paid groups of workers. By such machinery a basis is given to the wage system, but the super-structure includes rates for unskilled workers at a higher level than the minimum, and also rates for skilled workers of various grades. In certain industries it may be convenient to use minimum wage machinery to fix these higher rates. In others they may well be left, as a general rule, to the ordinary processes of collective bargaining, but where a collective agreement is of predominant importance in any industry the extension of its provisions to the whole of the industry may, in some cases, be desirable. Such an extension, by bringing the minority of an industry into line with the majority, would result in an increase in the standardisation of wage rates.

The above survey of methods of fixing minimum wages leads to the conclusion that the most satisfactory system may be that of the Central Commission. When fixing rates for any industry the Commission secures the advice of a representative board or conference of employers and workers. Greater co-ordination between rates in different industries is possible than under the Trade Boards system. If conditions justify such a course, the Commission may make periodic declarations of minimum rates of general application. If such general declarations are made, the Commission may also fix higher rates for various categories of workers in industries where regulation is not effected satisfactorily by collective agreement. In countries which have adopted compulsory arbitration there is a tendency for a single central body to declare basic minima, and also to make awards in cases of dispute. It is a convenient practice thus to combine the functions of a Central Commission with those of an Arbitration Court. In certain cases a Central Commission or other authority may find it desirable to take a collective agreement which covers some of the employers and workers in a trade and extend its provisions to the whole of the industry.

CHAPTER XI

METHODS OF ENFORCEMENT

THE fixing of legal minimum rates of wages involves the adoption of some method of ensuring that these rates are actually paid. This necessitates a system of discovering cases of non-observance ; also penalties must be imposed for non-compliance. Often methods of evasion, including collusion between employer and worker, render difficult the task of discovering defaulters. Miss Sells, in her book *The British Trade Boards System*, instances (p. 42) collusion between workers and employers in the chain trade at Cradley Heath, whereby the worker " gives overweight of chain, i.e. more than a hundredweight for the rate of a hundredweight, or returns part of his earnings in the form of a rebate." Experience in different countries shows that evasion and collusion are particularly widespread during periods of trade depression.

DISCOVERY OF DEFAULTERS.

For reporting cases of non-compliance it might be thought adequate if the workers themselves undertook such notification. The workers are acquainted with the rates of wages to which they are entitled, as minimum wage laws generally provide that employers shall post, in prominent places in the workshops, or

in places where work is given out, schedules showing
the minimum rates in force.   Failure on the part
of employers to post the schedules is generally punishable by fine.   Frequently, however, workers are afraid
to report their employers, as this might involve subsequent discrimination against them.   A number of
minimum wage laws provide for protection from
dismissal or other discrimination against workers who
give evidence of non-compliance on the part of their
employers ;   discrimination is usually punishable by
fine.   Such protection is necessary, but, nevertheless,
enforcement of minimum rates solely by the action
of individual workers would hardly give satisfactory
results.

Action for enforcing payment of the rates may be
taken by representatives of workers' organisations,
by employers, or by employers' associations.[1]   Thus
in the *Third Annual Report of the Ontario Minimum
Wage Board*, 1923 (p. 17), it is stated that "Many
of the complaints come directly from employees ;
others from their relatives or friends ;   others from
Trades and Labour Councils ;   others from social
workers, clergymen, or officials of the women's
organisations.   A number have come from employers.
Members of both the Provincial and Dominion Parlia-
ments have forwarded complaints."   In all countries
complaints received from such sources are valuable

---

[1] Mr. R. H. Tawney, in *Minimum Rates in the Chain-making
Industry*, describes (p. 127) how the Trade Union had established
a fairly elaborate system for detecting cases of underpayment.

means of discovering cases of non-observance. However, some more systematic method is required. Usually this is provided by the appointment of Government inspectors. Special inspectors may be appointed to enforce minimum wage orders, or this work may be undertaken by ordinary factory inspectors. In certain countries which have adopted the Central Commission system of fixing minimum wages, e.g. in some of the Provinces of Canada, special inspectors are appointed by the body which fixes the rates. Where the Trade Board system has been adopted, uniformity of enforcement can be ensured only if the task is undertaken by a central authority, and not separately by each Board. In Great Britain special inspectors of the Ministry of Labour undertake the task of enforcement. In Victoria the task forms part of the duties of the factory inspectorate.

Employers are required to keep registers showing the names of all workers in their employ who are covered by the minimum wage law, together with adequate records of the wages paid. These records are open to examination by inspectors. Failure to keep satisfactory records, or to submit them to inspection when required, generally involves liability to fine.

If enforcement is to be secured, the system of inspection must be adequate. In some countries complaints have been made that the inspectorate is too small to ensure observance of the law. Such complaints have been made in Great Britain. In 1922,

when the number of inspectors was 36, the Cave
Committee stated: " It is universally admitted that
it is wholly impossible for this small number of officers
to make inspections adequate for securing the Acts,
and much evasion is said to take place." At the end

	Year Ending December 31st.		
	1923.	1924.	1925.
Number of establishments on Trade Board lists on December 31st ..	180,641	171,540	155,350
Inspections—			
On complaint	1,091	1,717	2,646
Routine..	2,695	3,359 [1]	7,312 [1]
Total	3,786	5,076	9,958 [2]
Number of workers within scope of Trade Boards Acts in establishments inspected—			
On complaint	30,545	43,641	53,730
Routine..	35,513	45,065	57,636
Total	66,058	88,706	111,366

of 1923 the number of inspectors had been increased
to 40, and during 1924 sanction was obtained for a
permanent inspectorate of 60. At the end of 1925,
59 inspectors had been appointed and taken up work.

[1] Of these a certain number were made as a result of general
complaints against districts or groups of employers.

[2] Of these 6,550 were in establishments employing under
6 workers, 2,351 in establishments with 6–20 workers, 872
in establishments with 21–100 workers, and 185 in establishments with over 100 workers.

Nevertheless the number of establishments inspected during 1925 formed less than 6½ per cent. of the total number covered by the Acts. The table opposite shows the number of inspections made under the Trade Boards Acts during 1923, 1924, and 1925. It also indicates the importance of complaints made against defaulters as compared with routine inspections.[1]

PENALTIES FOR UNDERPAYMENT.

Two main types of penalty have been adopted, that of publicity and that of fines. Publicity as sole weapon has been tried only in Massachusetts, and the law of this State has attracted considerable attention on account of its unique character. Power is given to the wage-fixing authority to publish the names of employers whom it finds to be following or refusing to follow its wage recommendations.[2] During the early years of the law's operation, "white" lists of employers who paid the wage rates were sometimes published. Later, "black" lists of defaulters were published.[3] A section of the law provided that any newspaper refusing or neglecting to publish such a list of names, on payment of its regular rate for the space taken, would be liable to a fine. The constitutionality of this provision was challenged by the

[1] *Report of the Ministry of Labour for the Years 1923 and 1924* (Cd. 2481), and *for the Year 1925* (Cd. 2736).

[2] Failure of employers to post minimum wage decrees, to keep adequate wage records, or to submit such records to inspection is punishable by fine.

[3] *Monthly Labor Review*, August 1924, p. 294.

Boston Transcript Company, which had been fined
for refusing to publish a " black " list. The Supreme
Court of the State, to which the case was carried, gave
its decision in 1924 in favour of the Company.[1] Thus
the power to secure observance by means of the weapon
of publicity has been somewhat impaired. Now, the
only penalty for non-payment of the minimum rates
is advertisement in such newspapers as are willing
to publish lists, or in bulletins issued by the wage-
fixing authority.

Although the great majority of employers in Massachusetts in occupations for which wages have been
fixed have paid the rates recommended, the number
of cases of non-compliance has been considerable.
There was an important increase in non-observance
after 1920, when prices ceased to rise. As is indicated
in the *Reports of the Division of Minimum Wages of
the Department of Labor and Industries*, the rising
price-level during the period 1915 to 1920 facilitated
a high degree of observance, whereas the break in prices
in 1920 rendered enforcement difficult. In 1922 the
number of cases of non-compliance in twelve industries
was 5,675. More than 13 per cent. of women in the
firms inspected were receiving less than the decreed
minima.[2] It thus appears that the penalty of publicity
is inadequate. Also the pressure of public opinion or

[1] *Monthly Labor Review*, August 1924, pp. 174–5.

[2] Figures from the *American Economic Review*, March 1924,
p. 39, " A Recommendatory Minimum Wage Law : the first
decade of the Massachusetts Experiment," by Arthur Fletcher
Lucas.

of any boycott which the publication of a " black " list might stimulate bears unequally on different industries and occupations.   Where the good will of a firm is important, and where the employees are in direct contact with the consuming public, the penalty is severe.   Where the work is done through middlemen, publicity may have little effect.   Thus the 1921 *Report of the Minimum Wage Division* indicated that the penalty of publicity had proved unsatisfactory in the case of workers engaged in cleaning offices and other buildings.

The Massachusetts law has certainly led to an improvement in the conditions of women workers, but the improvement appears to have been due more to the willingness of many employers to co-operate than to fear of the penalty.   Against employers unwilling to co-operate a more severe penalty than publicity is necessary, especially as failure of some establishments to pay the minima may lead others, through fear of competition, to reduce their rates below the minima.   In view of these considerations the Massachusetts wage-fixing authority has endeavoured to secure an amendment of the law in order that contraventions would involve liability to fine. The State Legislature has not, however, made any change in this sense.[1]

[1] The Special Committee appointed by the Massachusetts Legislature in 1922 to examine the working of the minimum wage law recommended that the law should be continued in its present form for a further period.   (*Monthly Labor Review,* April 1923.)

In almost all States except Massachusetts failure to pay the mimimum wages fixed is punishable by fine.[1] In most cases also employers may be ordered to pay any balance of wages due to their workers, and the costs of the legal proceedings involved. However, although non-observance of minimum wage orders is almost universally punishable by fine, in most countries a policy of friendly adjustment is adopted, as far as possible, instead of prosecuting each employer who has paid wages below those fixed in the orders. Inspectors bring pressure on employers to pay arrears of wages and to avoid underpayment in future. Only recalcitrant employers are prosecuted. In a number of countries, including the United States, Canada, and Great Britain, prosecutions are rare. In Great Britain during the year 1925 the number of prosecutions for underpayment was only 23, although the number of establishments from which arrears of wages were claimed was 2,564.[2] From 1909 to the end of 1925 the total number of prosecutions, whether for underpayment or other causes, was only 184.

[1] In France no penalty is imposed for underpayment.
[2] *Report of the Ministry of Labour for the Year 1925*, (Cd. 2736), London, 1926.

CHAPTER XII

INTERNATIONAL ACTION

IN previous chapters attention has been directed solely to the fixing of minimum rates within any given country. International aspects of the problem are considered in the present chapter. Progress in the prevention of sweating and in raising the minimum standard of living of workers in some countries may be retarded, as a result of international competition, if similar advances are not made in other countries. This was recognised by the authors of the Treaty of Versailles. In Part XIII of the Treaty it is stated that the failure of any nation to secure to its workers an adequate living wage and other humane conditions of labour "is an obstacle in the way of other nations which desire to improve conditions in their own countries."

The competition of countries with lower standards has forced attention in advanced countries to the problem of protecting their higher labour standards. Also there is a desire to safeguard workers in backward countries against exploitation and misery. The main purpose of the present chapter is to indicate how these objects may be attained.

As a means of protecting the standards of one country against the lower standards of others the erection of a tariff barrier is sometimes proposed.[1] The case in favour of tariffs to protect the industries of any country generally includes the argument that its workers will be safeguarded against the competition of workers in countries with lower standards of labour. A general discussion of the advantages and disadvantages of protective tariffs is outside the scope of the present volume. On the special question of labour standards, tariffs may protect workers producing for the home market. To workers producing for foreign markets they are valueless as a safeguard against lower standards of labour conditions abroad.

Another proposal is for an international boycott to be organised against goods produced under " sweated " conditions.[2] A minimum standard of labour conditions would be established, and countries which were parties to the agreement would refuse to import goods produced under a lower standard. Evidently this plan might be applied with effect if such difficulties could be overcome as defining the minimum standard, securing satisfactory evidence that goods were being

[1] For example, the Austrian Chamber of Deputies, in 1924, passed a resolution by which import duties on goods from States whose hours of labour were considerably in excess of the standard set by the Washington Convention of 1919 could be increased by an amount not exceeding one-third. No action seems to have been taken to give effect to this resolution.

[2] This proposal is made in the Interim Report of the Sweated Goods Committee appointed by the Executive Committee of the British Parliamentary Labour Party. See *Sweated Imports and International Labour Standards*, published by the Labour Party, 1925.

produced at a lower standard, and finding an adequate number of countries to enforce the boycott. An international boycott is, however, an entreme measure which could rarely be applied.

Tariffs and boycotts are negative in character. On the positive side is action to secure greater standardisation of labour conditions in different countries. This method has received increased attention during recent years. A number of international organisations of workers have recognised its value. For example, the Committee of the International Miners' Federation, at a meeting held in Brussels in April 1925, considering that competition and commercial rivalry in the international coal market is more acute and embittered by reason of differences in the working conditions existing in the principal coal-producing countries, decided that efforts should be made to secure the standardisation of miners' working conditions on an international basis. The most potent instrument, however, for increasing the standardisation of labour conditions in different countries, and thus diminishing unfair competition resulting from unduly low standards in certain countries, is the International Labour Organisation. The activities of this organisation, in co-ordinating the labour legislation of different States, provide a means for greater international uniformity, and for attempting to secure that progress in improving labour conditions in some countries shall not be retarded by other nations lagging behind.

ACTION BY THE INTERNATIONAL LABOUR ORGANISATION.

Considerable progress has already been made by the International Labour Organisation in certain fields of labour legislation. In the case of minimum wages the Organisation, recognising the difficulties involved, has moved cautiously. In 1921 the Governing Body of the International Labour Office decided, on the proposal of Sir Malcolm Delevigne, the British Government Delegate, that the Office should undertake a documentary enquiry into the systems instituted by legislation in the different countries for regulating wages, more especially in industries in which the workers have little or no organisation, together with the results achieved. To give effect to this decision investigations were conducted into the minimum wage systems of countries in which developments were greatest.[1]

The favourable experience of these countries seemed to justify a consideration of the subject by the International Labour Conference, with a view to the adoption of a Draft Convention or Recommendation. Consequently, in January 1926, on the proposal of Mr. Humbert Wolfe, British Government Delegate, the Governing Body agreed to place the following item on the agenda of the 1927 Conference :—

Minimum wage fixing machinery in trades in which organisation of employers and workers is defective, and

---

[1] The results of these investigations were published in a series of articles in the *International Labour Review.*

where wages are exceptionally low, with special reference to the homeworking trades.[1]

In placing this subject on the agenda the purpose is the adoption of a Draft Convention or Recommendation inviting each Government to set up machinery for fixing minimum wages in certain trades. There is no intention of attempting to establish an international minimum wage. This is in conformity with the principles laid down in the Peace Treaty to guide the policy of the International Labour Organisation. The principles include " payment to the employed of a wage adequate to maintain a reasonable standard of life as this is understood in their time and country." It has been seen that the amount necessary to maintain a reasonable standard of life varies from one country to another. The Conference would, therefore, merely indicate the main features of the system, and machinery set up in each country would fix minimum rates according to the special circumstances of the time and country. The general view of the Governing Body appears to be that States should not interfere in the regulation of wages if there is a reasonable chance that employers and workers can effect such regulation for themselves by collective agreement. Also there should be interference with freedom in fixing wages only to prevent hardship resulting from exceptionally low wages.

[1] Earlier proposals of a similar character had been postponed owing to the prevalence of unstable economic conditions in certain countries, and also because further investigation of the problem was considered necessary.

Each country would determine for itself the industries in which wages are unduly low, and where organisation among the employers and workers is inadequate to ensure the satisfactory regulation of wages by collective agreements. It follows that uniformity of application of the Draft Convention or Recommendation in different countries would be attained only if each country were to adopt similar criteria for determining the industries in which organisation is defective and wages unduly low.

Organisation in any trade might be considered defective if less than a given proportion of all workers in the trade were members of a Trade Union. Another test is the proportion of workers covered by collective agreements in force. This would give a better indication than membership of effectiveness of organisation in regulating conditions of labour. Wages in any trade might be regarded as exceptionally low if they were less than an agreed percentage of the average wage of unskilled workers in specified industries. The percentage and the specified industries would be included in the international agreement. The establishment and application of such criteria for determining defectiveness of organisation and exceptionally low wages would be far from easy, but to have no agreed criteria would almost certainly result in unequal application of the Draft Convention or Recommendation in different countries.

The adoption by the International Labour Conference of a Draft Convention or Recommendation on such lines would ensure consideration of the question by Parliament, or other competent authority, in each country, and would thus provide a stimulus to the setting up of machinery for fixing minimum wages.[1] There is a real need for effective minimum wage machinery to be set up in industrial countries which have not yet adopted the system. These countries would gain by an improvement in the standard of living of their lowest paid groups of workers. In effecting this improvement they would benefit from the experience in administration of minimum wage legislation in countries which have been pioneers of the system. The pioneer countries would themselves benefit from the protection which the general establishment of minimum wage fixing machinery would provide, by the removal of unfair competition of low-paid labour in other countries.

It would be desirable that each country which applied the minimum wage Convention or Recommendation should publish information showing the trades for which minimum wages were regulated and the rates fixed. This, together with information regarding enforcement, would provide a basis for determining effectiveness of application.

---

[1] By Article 405 of the Treaty of Versailles, States which are members of the International Labour Organisation undertake to bring Recommendations or Draft Conventions before the competent authority within a period generally of one year from the termination of the Conference at which they were adopted. The competent authority in any country is free either to give effect to such Recommendations or Draft Conventions, or to reject them.

IS AN INTERNATIONAL MINIMUM WAGE PRACTICABLE ?

It has been seen that any action which the International Labour Organisation is likely to take in the early future with regard to the minimum wage question will not aim at uniformity of rates. This is in keeping with the intention of the authors of the labour provisions of the Peace Treaty. They recognised that in applying various principles of labour legislation " differences of climate, habits, and customs, of economic opportunity and industrial tradition, make strict uniformity in the conditions of labour difficult of immediate attainment."

With regard to some conditions of labour uniform international standards may readily be adopted. Thus rights of association may be secured, child labour and night work of women may be abolished, and a weekly rest of at least twenty-four hours established for all workers. In the case of minimum wages there is no possibility of an early establishment of international uniformity. This is evident from the figures given in the table opposite. They are index numbers of real wages calculated by comparing the purchasing power of wages in different cities over certain food budgets representative of the consumption of workers in different countries, allowance being made for rent. As no account is taken of expenditure on clothing, fuel, light, and various other items of importance in the consumption of the workers, the index numbers imperfectly represent the relative levels of real wages. They do, however, indicate how considerable are the differences. For example, the index number for Philadelphia is about 70 per cent. higher than that for London, and more than three times that for Vienna.

INDEX NUMBERS OF COMPARATIVE REAL WAGES IN VARIOUS CITIES AT THE BEGINNING OF APRIL 1926.[1]

(*Base :* LONDON = 100).

City.	Index Number.	City.	Index Number.
Philadelphia ..	168	Stockholm ..	85
Ottawa ..	143	Berlin	66
Sydney ..	130	Paris	61
London ..	100	Prague	58
Oslo	100[2]	Brussels ..	56
Amsterdam ..	88	Vienna	50

[1] *International Labour Review*, July 1926. The figures cover typical categories of workers in the building, metal, furniture-making, printing and bookbinding industries. The data on which the index numbers are based are wages for a week of forty-eight hours at ordinary time rates. The method of calculation is described in detail in the *International Labour Review* for October 1924 and subsequent numbers. The figures show similar results to those calculated by the British Ministry of Labour and published in the *Labour Gazette* from July 1923 to June 1924.

It should be noted that the index numbers do not show differences in the general level of wages, even in the cities included, being based on the wages of a few categories of workers only. They are still less representative of differences in the levels of real wages in the various countries. They serve, however, as a rough indication of the relative levels of real wages of adult male workers in certain occupations and cities in different countries.

[2] The figure for Oslo is exceptionally high as a result of a rise in the value of the Norwegian crown.

The range would be even greater if similar statistics were available also for countries such as India and China.

Some of the differences shown in the table on page 189 may be due to factors of a temporary character. For example, real wages in certain Central European countries are lower relatively to those in other countries at the present time than they were before the war, but there are indications that they are likely to rise again to a level nearer to that in Western European and Scandinavian countries.[1] Other differences, however, appear to be due to causes of a more permanent character, e.g. the effects of variations in climate, in economic resources, in physiological requirements, and in efficiency. These factors are reflected in total output, and in the long run a country can consume only that which it produces, no more, no less. The more permanent inequalities imply that international uniformity of minimum wages is quite impracticable.[2] If the minimum wage were based on conditions in countries in which wages are lowest, it would be valueless for countries with higher

[1] According to calculations made before the war by the British Board of Trade, the relation between real wages in England and Germany was 100 : 73.

[2] A case might be made out for equality of piece rates of wages in various countries, although inequalities in efficiency would mean that earnings would differ. It would be necessary, however, to take account of differences in machinery and conditions of work in various countries, as equality of piece rates is justifiable only if methods of production are similar.

standards; on the other hand, it would be impossible to apply in backward countries the wage standards of the leading industrial States.

Nor is the adoption of an international minimum wage necessary to adjust conditions of international competition. Real wages in the United States, for example, are considerably higher than in Germany, and international trade is already largely adjusted to these differences. If, by the application of minimum wage machinery, the wages of the lowest paid groups of workers in *both* countries are raised simultaneously by, say, 10 per cent., there will be little or no change in the relative power of the two countries in the international market. If, however, one country fails to advance at about the same rate as the other, the balance may be disturbed, and social progress in the second country hindered by the increased competitive power of the first. The establishment in all countries of effective minimum wage fixing machinery, on the lines indicated in the preceding section, would remove this danger by securing to the lowest paid groups of workers a wage not unduly low in relation to the general standard of each country.

The standards of different countries are, however, continually changing, and, with the development of international trade, increased mobility of labour, and the extension of advanced methods of production to hitherto backward countries, the tendency is in the direction of less inequalities. Western countries will not be able to maintain permanently their present *relative* advantages.   There is no reason why Western standards should fall, or why, if the progress of industrial development continues, those standards should not rise, but the rise in so-called backward countries is likely to be relatively greater.

The tendency is, therefore, for real wages to be less unequal in the future, though even in the distant future, a uniform minimum wage, applicable in all countries, is improbable.   It may be possible, however, for agreements to be reached by groups of nations in which economic conditions are similar for the adoption of a common standard or standards.   Such possible developments are foreshadowed to some extent by the similarity of minimum rates fixed in various States in the United States, in Australia, and in Canadian Provinces.[1]   There are certain groups of countries in which economic conditions are at least as similar as those in different parts of Canada, Australia, or the United States, and in the future it may be feasible for agreement on common standards of minimum wages to be reached between countries in such groups.   In the case of countries with different wage standards agreement might be reached for the minimum wage in each country to be fixed at a given proportion of the average wage of unskilled workers in specified industries.   International agreement would determine

---

[1] In Canada proposals have been made for an inter-provincial conference with the object of securing the adoption of more uniform minimum wage machinery in the different Provinces.   A further development might be agreement on uniform minimum wages.

the industries to be included when calculating the average wage of unskilled workers in each country, and the percentage below this average at which the minimum should be fixed. The minimum in any country would be determined according to its own standards.

INDEX

For Product Safety Concerns and Information please contact our EU
representative GPSR@taylorandfrancis.com Taylor & Francis Verlag GmbH,
Kaufingerstraße 24, 80331 München, Germany

Printed and bound by CPI Group (UK) Ltd, Croydon, CR0 4YY
08/05/2025
01864366-0003